John and Carol and friends from Romford

Thank you for sharing our celebration and we look forward to coming to Romford.

Peter Munn

CAPTAIN

Kath Buckley

Ladies Captain

CHISLEHURST
GOLF CLUB

125 years at Camden Place

OCBC

Old Chapel Books, Chislehurst

Published in Great Britain by
Old Chapel Books, Chislehurst,
The Old Chapel, Queens Passage, Chislehurst, BR7 5AP

Published March 2019

ISBN 978-1-912236-13-8

Printed in Great Britain by
CPI Antony Rowe Ltd

Designed by Mary & Mick Design
www.maryandmick.com

Picture Acknowledgements
The publisher wishes to thank the organisations and individuals
for their kind permission to reproduce
the photographs and illustrations in this book.

A foreword from the Senior Past Captain

I t is a privilege to be asked to write a foreword to this book celebrating 125 years of Chislehurst Golf Club. The Club was founded at the time of an explosion of new golf clubs at the end of the 19th century. One thousand new clubs were formed over a period of ten years, yet of the one hundred formed in 1894 only thirty two survived to celebrate their centenary. Chislehurst, which was opened by the right Honourable A.J. Balfour, Captain of the Royal &Ancient (R&A) and Prime Minister in 1902, is one that has continued, on the same site, although enlarged from its original nine-hole format.

Credit must be paid to those individuals whose foresight helped establish and protect the Club over the years, and whose early actions prevented Camden Park becoming a housing estate and to those who found ways for the club to be owned by its members. Generations of those members have taken on roles as club and company officials for no reward other than the satisfaction of helping keep Chislehurst a great golf club to be associated with. Thanks and appreciation go to them all.

Chislehurst has from early days been a family club encouraging the instruction of young people in the technique of the game together with its etiquette. This has remained its ethos and it is hoped that it will continue in future years. Since the opening in 1894 when Tom Dunn created not just the 9-hole course but a specific course for the ladies, our female members have been central to the success of the club both on and off the golf course and the club's stars over the years have numbered **as** many ladies as men.

We are privileged to have as our clubhouse the magnificent building with its fascinating history. It is the envy of many visitors. It was thought appropriate to bring the history of the Club up to date by adding to the definitive works of Bill Mitchell and Donald Sim, published to coincide with the centenary in 1994. This book presents some of the history along with a summary of what has happened in the following years. Chislehurst is a special Club and in the future I hope that it will continue to prosper in a similar way, enabling its members to enjoy golf and relaxation amongst friends and their families in fine surroundings.

Dr John Williams: *Captain 1973 and Senior Past Captain from 2018*

Thank you

Many people have helped shape this book. Internally thanks must go to the Board who supported the idea and to all those members who looked out old photos and shared their anecdotes and memories. Three past Chairmen Michael Hollingsworth, John Lenton and Michael Lodwig provided us with recollections of their time in office; Ken Stone revisited the centenary celebrations; Bob Matthews worked on plans to illustrate the evolution of Camden Place over some 300 years; Gordon Caldwell and Ian Page provided support throughout.

We had external help as well: Joanna Friel and the Chislehurst Society; Bromley Library who gave us permission to use Ken Wilson's work on Camden Place; our designer Mick Pearce who contributed a number of images; Coopers School students, under the guidance of their teacher Nick Johnson, produced some inspirational photographs to supplement the work contributed by our own Steve Jones, Eric Coburn, Alex Shipman and the many members who opened their family albums for us. Eric Pape took on the challenge of being our critical reader and Pat Waters was our patient proof-reader; Tony Allen from Old Chapel Books gave us professional guidance and introduced us to our designers and printer. Our thanks go to all of them.

It is to three people, sadly no longer with us, to whom we owe the greatest debt. Donald Sim, Captain 1974, undertook the lion's share of the historical research into Camden Place and the creation of the Golf Club. His groundwork and inspiration allowed Bill Mitchell, Captain 1991, to add the golfing history of the Club and create *Chislehurst Golf Club*, the book published for the centenary in 1994. It is testament to their work that we have added very little to their fact base. We have instead been able to borrow from them and with the benefits of digital printing and new technology to include many more images, adding another dimension to their narrative. The third person to be acknowledged is Ken Wilson, the designer of Bromley's Churchill Theatre. Ken wrote and illustrated the *Camden Place Story*. His insight and drawings bring the earliest days of Camden Place to life.

We hope you enjoy the result of these collective efforts.

Angela Hatton   Steve Jones   David Hatton

An Introduction

Today the trees are more mature and there are more houses to be seen between them but Camden Place is still a surprisingly tranquil corner of Chislehurst. The Club has survived bombings and financial crises, it has witnessed the changing popularity of the game of golf but throughout it has remained a course that members and visitors love. Although short in length, it challenges the accuracy of the best players and the parkland setting is something special. At its core is a magnificent clubhouse with a history worth recalling and preserving.

This book was compiled to help mark 125 years of golf at Chislehurst and celebrate the work of the many members, who over the years have made CGC what it is today. We hope it provides you with a sense of the history of both Camden Place and Chislehurst Golf Club and the images and stories we have shared give clues as to why the Club has stood the test of time.

Section 1 takes you on a whistle-stop tour of the evolution of Camden Place, a building dating back to 1717, which has been remodelled as a country house, a Georgian mansion and a French château. It has been the scene of murder and the home of the French Court. Politicians and royalty have visited and it has played a key role in the economic development and social life of Chislehurst.

Section 2 focuses on the birth of the Golf Club. Snatched from the hands of developers by the work of the Commons Conservators, led by Alexander Travers Hawes, the first golf course comprised 9 holes but the Club also boasted a ladies' course. The design and then development of 18 holes and the transition from a proprietors' club to a private and then members owned club is quite a tale featuring a cast of players.

Section 3 charts the first 125 years of CGC. We have picked some anecdotes, images, details and successes to give you a flavour of past events, dramas and challenges on and off the course. Our apologies in advance for those we left out.

It is our hope that many future generations of members, friends and visitors are able to enjoy a drink on the Jubilee Terrace, watching the sun set across our course. It is a perfect end to a summer's day and a special pleasure that CGC members are privileged to enjoy and one of which it is impossible to tire.

Contents

THE LATE PRINCE

Presented to CHIS

1

The Story of Camden Place

Camden Place has a history that can be traced back to the early 1600's when antiquarian William Camden built a home on the site. Parts of the current building go back to 1717 but since then it has gone through several transformations, from country house to Georgian mansion, French château and finally a unique clubhouse for Chislehurst Golf Club. This first section tells something of that journey.

Photo by Bailey Bellenie, Coopers School

Early days of Chislehurst

Chislehurst's name has Anglo Saxon roots and a history that can be tracked back to 1089 when Gundolph, the Bishop of Rochester, granted the monks of the Cathedral Priory the right to select a rector for Chislehurst.

The town developed as four quite separate 'villages', located around the Common. There was the High Street known as Prickend, Village Street, which would later become Royal Parade, built around the Bull's Head Inn, and Mill Place which included Camden Place and Perry Street.

The arrival of William Camden

Located just over ten miles south east of Charing Cross, Chislehurst's proximity to London explains its growth and development over the years

In the late 16th century, as the air pollution in London worsened and the first outbreaks of plague occurred, the wealthy looked for a healthier and more comfortable place to call home. Chislehurst was ideal, conveniently located for both the Royal household at Greenwich and the City.

In 1609 one such newcomer was William Camden (1551-1623). He was already something of a celebrity, a famous historian, author and academic. Camden, who was unmarried, built himself a house on or near the current location of Camden Place. Situated in 1½– 2 acres, it was a substantial property surrounded on three sides by the Common.

The Common is central to the Golf Club story. It was through enclosure of the Common that expansion of the Camden estate was possible and the Golf Club only came into existence because in 1893 the Commons Conservators used the 'rights of way' they controlled to save the Camden Park Estate from being developed for housing.

No pictures of the original house exist but Ken Wilson in his work *Camden Place Story* provided this depiction of what it may have looked like.

© Bromley Library

1609
William Camden
moves to Chislehurst

Camden's Achievements

Camden achieved a great deal: he was a very successful Headmaster at Westminster School, the Librarian of Westminster Abbey between 1587 and 1597 and author of a number of books including a Greek grammar, the first guidebook of the monuments of Westminster Abbey and his renowned book *Britannia* (a description of Britain and Ireland) which went into many editions. His final work, written whilst he was at Chislehurst, was the *Annals of Queen Elizabeth*.

Although a layman he was appointed the Prebend of Ilfracombe at Salisbury Cathedral and in 1597 Clarenceux King of Arms, one of the three offices of the College of Arms. The *Camden Chair of Ancient History* at the University of Oxford was established in 1622 by him, making it the first and today the oldest chair of history in England.

Camden wanted to *'be buried in that place where it should please god to call me to his mercye'*. However on his death in 1623 this request was ignored by his friends and he was buried in Westminster Abbey, not Chislehurst, his contributions now celebrated at Poets' Corner.

1623
William Camden dies
and buried at
Poets' Corner

William Camden's memorial
© Westminster Abbey

The building of Camden House

After Camden's death his house had a succession of owners but in the early 18th century the property was bought by Robert Weston, who set about building a new L-shaped country house in the grounds. He named it *Camden House*, creating a permanent link to the famous early owner of the land.

Weston probably took the magnificent Jacobean wood panelling for the entrance hall from another building and it is possible that it came from the original William Camden house. It is still in situ and the oak details and carvings are well worth a second look.

There are two 'secret doors' in the panelling. They provided discrete access to the dining- and sitting-rooms located either side of the hall, so would have been used mainly by the servants.

Weston's new house was just the starting point in developing the property as we know it now. Two major transformations would occur before becoming Chislehurst's clubhouse. Today the original Weston accommodations are the 'west wing' of the property, consisting of the committee room, club office, kitchens and store rooms.

CAMDEN HOUSE 1717
SITE LAYOUT / WESTON'S HOUSE / CAMDEN'S HOUSE / N

After Weston's death the house had a number of owners before being bought by Charles Pratt.

13

Weston's avenue of trees

Weston wanted an entrance worthy of his new property. To create this he needed to enclose about one acre of the Common. He approached the Vestry for a lease, which was granted for a term of 500 years on 17 June 1718. In exchange he provided three shillings of rent to the Lord of the Manor and nine shillings, payable to the Church Wardens, to be used for the poor of the parish.

The enclosed land ran southwards from the south side of Camden Place towards the public road from Bromley (now Old Hill). On this land he planted an avenue of trees, three deep on the west side of the path leading to the house and two deep on the east.

Camden Park Road did not exist then and the drive protruded further than today but did not extend quite as far as the public road. A strip of the common was left between the enclosed land and the public road. This strip of common land would be crucial in later battles to stop the developers building their housing estate on Camden Park.

1718
Enclosure of
1 acre
of common land

Charles Pratt - Lord Camden

Charles Pratt was born in 1714 and purchased *Camden House* in 1760, renaming it *Camden Place*. He was an ambitious and radical lawyer and by 1765 was Attorney General and Lord Chief Justice, a post his father had also held. In 1776 when he became Lord Chancellor he was made an Earl and took the title *Baron Camden of Camden Place*.

His choice of title was an unusual departure. According to the late Sir Gerald Wollaston, sometime Garter King of Arms, '*It was an astonishing thing and without precedent that a man should be allowed to take another man's surname as his title, but that is what happened.*'

Enclosing the Common

Lord Camden set about a huge programme of work and expansion that would last 25 years. He bought a large tract of land to the west of the estate, known as Red Hill Wood, from the executors of Thomas Farringdon. He converted part of this into a park. Today this is the golf course. The remainder he renamed Camden Wood.

He enclosed two pieces of the Common, a narrow strip of just over one acre, covering the whole eastern frontage of the house and a further 2 acres to the north of the property. He wanted to go further but when he tried to acquire more of the Common, a parish meeting raised strong objections and the Vestry stopped him. He seems to have taken this rebuff well and is reported as saying, '*Lord Camden has received too much from the Parish already to take it amiss or be displeased with such refusal*'.

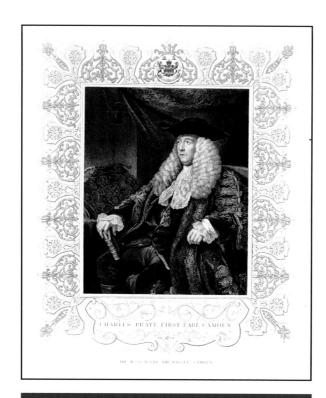

Lord Camden's expansion activity did however inspire a pithy poem condemning the English enclosure movement – the process of fencing off common land and turning it into private property.

T'is bad enough in man or woman
To steal a goose from off the common
But surely he's without excuse
Who steals the common from the goose.

A Commonplace Book of Epigrams
by Charles Stokes Carey 1872

1760
Camden House is bought
by Charles Pratt

From country house to Georgian mansion

Weston's L-shaped property was just the starting point for Lord Camden. He appointed George Dance R.A. the renowned architect, and together they transformed the house, significantly expanding the property. Its Georgian exterior was in the classical style introduced 100 years earlier by Inigo Jones.

The original Weston building was largely turned into service accommodation and a three storey frontage was built on the east side of the old house. A two storey wing was added on the south. Upstairs there were now eight bedrooms with dressing-rooms and sitting-rooms, whilst the third floor had enough space for ten servants.

The house was given its grand drawing-room and two entrance halls, one the oak-panelled entrance which led from the pleasure gardens, the other, the main entrance and staircase which would later become the Oval Room.

Ice-house or bath-house?

Hidden in the copse beside the Temple there lurks a circular building with several features which suggest it may have once been an ice-house. It is, however, described in the Ordnance Survey map of 1865 as an engine-house. The engine would presumably have pumped water from the well within the Temple for use in the oblong bath-house marked out further down the 15th fairway, no mean trek from the mansion on bath nights in the winter! The bath-house still features in a map of 1875 but no trace of it remained by the time the golfers arrived in 1894.

Changing owners

One year after inheriting Camden Place from his cousin, John Jeffrey Pratt (later to become the first Marquess of Camden) sold Camden Place to Stephen Lushington who kept the property until 1805.

1794
Lord Camden dies

1795
Camden Place
was sold
to Lushington

The Bonar years and murders

Thomson Bonar was a wealthy merchant who owned the mansion and farm at Elmstead. In 1805 he purchased Camden Estate. He and his wife Anne had two sons and a grandson. They were a close couple who would live and die together in Camden Place.

Inside, the south entrance to the house was closed and rounded off and the main stairs were moved, creating the Oval Room. This room now became a library with the book shelves still in place behind the Dutch murals. A new dining-room was added (which would later become the billiard-room) and a large kitchen block built where the men's locker rooms are today.

Outside new outbuildings were added in an area which is now covered by Wilderness Road. There were two carriage houses each with three bays and stabling for 18 horses. There were new staff quarters for 30, a gardener's cottage, offices, workshops, a dairy and cow sheds.

The murders

On Sunday 31 May 1813, a footman in the house, Irish-born Philip Nicholson, brutally murdered Anne and Thomson Bonar in their beds. The murders were apparently motiveless but Nicholson admitted them and was tried at Maidstone assizes. He was found guilty and sentenced to hang at Penenden Heath. It seems he had a hard death. After hanging an hour his body was put into a post-chaise and driven to Bromley. There he was dissected by Dr James Scott.

Anne and Thomson were buried together. Their tomb inscription near the lych-gate in St Nicholas' churchyard, describes their deaths as 'a signal reward for such virtues as have rarely been united' and in accord with 'their fervent wish, so frequently expressed and so mysteriously fulfilled, that they might leave this world together'.

THE DAIRY AND STABLES ·

1813
The Bonars
are murdered

Tenants and a French connection

After the Bonars' deaths the house was used by their son and subsequently let by him to a stream of tenants including a Mr Henry Rowles, a Middlesex J.P. who was Chairman of the Globe Insurance and builder of Drury Lane Theatre. His wife was of Spanish origin and in her prime is said to have been one of the loveliest women in Europe. Their daughter Emily was born at Camden Place in 1823 and inherited her mother's beauty. In her teens Emily was enthusiastically courted by the then exiled Prince Louis Napoleon who was later to become Emperor Napoleon lll.

The Rowles had left Camden Place when Emily was two years old, so the courtship did not include visits to Chislehurst but it does seem to have been a serious relationship and it is not too far-fetched to imagine conversations about Chislehurst and Camden Place. There were extravagant gifts and talk of an engagement but the courtship ended abruptly in 1840, when the young Prince set out on an ill-fated journey from Gravesend to Boulogne with the intention of persuading the French people to reinstate the Napoleonic dynasty. His quest failed and he was arrested, tried in Paris and sentenced to perpetual imprisonment in the Castle of Ham on the Somme. Emily Rowles stayed in touch during his imprisonment and their friendship continued when he escaped after six years. Although the friendship lasted, the romance was not rekindled, possibly because Emily knew that during his incarceration at Ham, Louis Napoleon had an affair with a pretty laundress, Alexandrine Vergeot, and had two sons with her. These sons were made Counts in 1870 when Napoleon was Emperor. Napoleon seems to have been able to maintain his connections with 'old friends'. When Emily Rowles died in 1876 as the widowed Marchesa Campana, she was still in receipt of a French state pension.

Emily Rowles
Illustration by Ken Wilson

1860 a Sham Fight in Chislehurst

On 14 July there was an unusual event, worthy as a footnote in our history. A Sham Fight was held on the grounds of Camden Place, involving thousands of volunteers and onlookers. This was an unusual spectacle which attracted considerable interest locally. Its purpose was serious, to practise battle strategies.

Some 100 Metropolitan Police officers were conveyed by train to the nearest station, Bickley (then Southborough Road), which had been opened in 1858. These officers were placed along the road between the railway station and Camden Park with the Divisional horse-drawn 'Black Maria' stationed on Chislehurst Common to convey those arrested to the station-house at St Mary Cray. In addition about a dozen plain-clothes men were deployed amongst the spectators. Clearly crowd trouble was anticipated.

The battle was described thus:-

The force of over 8,000 soldiers was divided into 2 divisions, one for attack and one for defence.

The army of attack was commanded by Lord Radstock and Lord Bury and the defending force by Colonel G M Hicks and Col. the Hon. C H Lindsay.

There were 3 separate lines of attack and defence, the first commencing on the Chislehurst Road and resulting in the repulse and retreat of the defending party through the valley and up the sloping hill in Camden Park.

At the corner of the hill the tables were to be turned and the attacking party were to be driven back in confusion down the hill. After being repulsed the attacking columnists were to reform in the valley and resume the attack by a flank movement.

Ultimately the whole force bivouacked on the slope of a hill in the park which presented a most favourable opportunity for that purpose, with the Ravensbourne, a clear and sparkling brook running at its base.

Extract from a flier promoting the Sham Fight

From Georgian mansion to French château

In 1860 Camden Place once more found an enthusiastic owner with a new, somewhat surprising, vision for the property. This owner, Nathaniel William Strode, set about transforming the Georgian mansion into a semblance of a French château. His motives for doing this are not certain. It was claimed he had a premonition that his friend the Emperor Napoleon III may one day need a bolt-hole in England, a possibility in light of the uncertainty of French politics. An alternative version is Strode simply appreciated French style and created the house to suit his own tastes. Strode had his own crest carved into the pediment at the front of the building – his motto (loosely translated) *'death before dishonour.'*

A third, more pragmatic explanation may be that Strode was acting as an agent for Napoleon and he was paid to prepare the property for any future possible exile. This motive gained credibility once it became known that 900,000 francs was paid to Strode from the French Civil List.

21

1860
Bought by
Nathaniel
William Strode

The Strode/Napoleon connection

Strode had become friendly with Prince Louis Napoleon after his return to England in 1846, following his escape from the Castle at Ham.

Strode at that time was trustee for a very wealthy lady, Elizabeth Anne Haryett, who changed her name to Miss Howard. She was an actress and a red-haired beauty who had a long lasting liaison with the Prince. She was generous with her money (gained from a succession of suitors and lovers) and she provided financial support for Napoleon's political ambitions in France.

When he returned to France in 1848 and became President, she set herself up in a house in Paris and a flat at Saint-Cloud. Here she was able to discretely look after the two sons, born to Napoleon whilst imprisoned at Ham. They acted as companions to her own son. Napoleon ended the affair with Miss Howard in 1852 just before his marriage to another red-head, Eugénie de Montijo. A disappointed Miss Howard was mollified with the title of Comtesse de Beauregard and an estate near Versailles.

It is a possibility that the mysterious 900,000 franc payment to Strode was in fact a repayment entrusted to him on behalf of Miss Howard.

A château in Chislehurst

Whatever the motivation, over ten years, under Strode's direction, Camden Place was remodelled, extended and furnished, creating a property fit for an Emperor and Empress.

To achieve this transformation Strode made many changes. Bonar's modest dining-room became a billiard-room. A second protruding wing was added, becoming the new dining-room. This room was built to the precise measurements required to accommodate the unaltered 18th century wood panelling that came from the Château de Brécy. The château was a hunting lodge near Compiègne which had been owned by a member of the Bourbon family and was demolished in 1861. As a result of the panelling being installed unaltered two of the doors, which presumably led to rooms in the hunting lodge, open onto a brick wall in Camden Place.

European furnishings and fittings were obtained including the fleur-de-lis fireback in what is now the front office. Murals and art works were added. Some of the murals can still be seen in situ but when the contents of Camden Place were sold at auction by Christies following Strode's death in 1889, 110 lots of artwork went under the hammer. There were also 46 tapestries. One of them was described as 'a fine oblong panel of old Brussels tapestry representing a Kermeese village, numerous figures and landscape in background with a scroll border'. It measured 11 foot four inches by 19 foot 6 inches and sold for £472 10s the equivalent of approximately £53,500 in 2018.

It is also assumed that Strode installed the oval French painting above the main stairs depicting Leda and the Swan. Sotheby's described the ceiling work as 'School of Boucher - oil on canvas, oval inset in ceiling'. Boucher was a French painter and engraver who was born in 1703 and died in Paris is 1770.

Photo by Alissa Bowley
Coopers School

22

The Strode gates to Camden Place:
image provided by the Chislehurst Society

A grand façade

Outside, the stone balustrade parapet with decorative urns gave the building a more regal look. The whole external appearance was altered to match the style of the new dining-room to the right. A brick facing was built around Lord Camden's three-storey central block and Thomson Bonar's eating-room.

A lot of ornamentation was added. A gilt clock, bas-relief sculpture and terra–cotta panels were added to the main entrance and over the window heads. As today, Grecian style vases flanked the entrance and there was a large conservatory which projected out from the south elevation.

A new wide drive was laid out alongside Robert Weston's tree-lined drive and the pleasure garden was replaced with a turning circle for coaches. The beautiful Strode gates were added. Many of these changes have remained and still give the building a French character. The original Camden Place gates came from the Paris Exposition of 1867 and were part of the Strode transformation. In this image you can just see the corner of one of the four roomed lodges Strode erected just inside the gates, which were further forward than today's entrance.

A second lodge was built at the northern entrance to the estate at the end of what is now Wilderness Road. This entrance led to a right of way across the common to the public road, now Prince Imperial Road.

There are two versions of how the gates came to Chislehurst. The straightforward version is that they were bought by Strode himself. The alternative is that Napoleon acquired them and sent them as a gift to his ex-mistress Miss Howard, who gave the gates to Strode. In either case, the gates survived until early 1943 when they were taken away for the war effort.

The Temple

Perhaps the most unusual addition to Camden Place was the well-head on the right of the 15th fairway. It is said to be a copy of one in the park at the Château de Saint-Cloud, a suburb of Paris and a favourite location of Napoleon. If it was added to make the French family feel at home, it seems to have been a success.

Originally the CGC Temple was more ornate with six vertical wooden columns, engaged from the base to the roof around the outside of the structure as well as a wooden door. Over the years these rotted and were removed after 1945. It is still a focal point and since 1953 has been the symbol of the Club. The Temple Trophy is a silver replica of the Temple and is contested for in an annual foursomes match.

'But the thing which above all thrilled Louis (the Prince Imperial) was an object they saw standing in a hollow in the park. It was a small, odd stone erection of classical design. Louis could hardly believe his eyes and stopped dead in his tracks. He recognised it at once – it was the Lantern of Demosthenes. The past rushed up before him. There was a Lantern of Demosthenes in the park at Saint-Cloud. It was amazing that he should have come all this way to find the Lantern waiting for him. From that moment Louis decided that Camden Place was not so bad.'

The Prince Imperial, a study of his life among the British:
E.E.P. Tisdall -1959.

The Saint-Cloud Temple was itself a copy and the design of the original temple can be dated back 2,500 years to the Choragic Monument of Lysicrates, which stood on the slopes of the Athenian Acropolis. In 1770 James 'Athenian' Stuart constructed an accurate copy of the Monument in the grounds of Shugborough Place in Staffordshire and known as the Lanthorn of Demosthenes.

Bailey Bellenie

Alissa Bowley

In 2018 the Chislehurst Society's Environmental Awards were themed Imperial Chislehurst.

The photography students from Coopers School under their tutor Nick Johnson visited Camden Place and took pictures using a variety of techniques.

Imperial Chislehurst

By the end of 1870 Strode's premonition and concern about the fragile politics in France proved true. An unwell Napoleon lll took on the Prussian army at Sedan on 1 September in an attempt to prevent the Germans besieging Paris. It was a bloody battle and he was soundly defeated. It is estimated that 3,000 French were killed, 14,000 wounded and 103,000 captured at the Battle of Sedan. The Germans lost 2,320, with 5,980 wounded and 700 missing. Napoleon's hope of dying in a second wave of attack and preserving his honour was thwarted because he was in such pain with his bladder stones he had to be removed from the field. He surrendered and was imprisoned.

Empress Eugénie, fleeing the resulting riots in Paris, arrived in England and was joined by the Prince Imperial, who at 14 had been sent away from the battlefield at Sedan for his safety. Strode was quick to put the house at their disposal. Together Eugénie and the Prince made their way to Chislehurst, a welcome sanctuary perhaps but it must have seemed bleak on a wet winter's day in Kent.

Queen Victoria made an early visit to Eugénie on the 30 November 1870. It was a dull, raw, winter's day. And Victoria wrote in her diary:
'At the door stood the poor Empress in black, the Prince Imperial and, a little behind, the ladies and gentlemen. Everything was like a French house and there were many pretty things about. She looks thin and pale but still very handsome. The Prince Imperial is a nice boy but rather short and stumpy. We stayed about half an hour. It was a sad visit and seemed like a strange dream.'

The Prince's tutor Augustin Filon described the arrival at Camden Place of Eugénie and Prince Imperial in 1870:

'On entering the house I found myself in a large corridor facing a big hall where the light falls through a skylight. On the walls of the hall and along those of the corridor were pictures, busts and cabinets of ebony or tortoiseshell inlaid with mother-of-pearl, brass and copper; behind the glass doors of these cabinets was arranged a vast and heterogeneous collection of objects of very unequal value. At the end of the hall was a huge bevelled mirror with a carved and pierced frame. To the right a big gilded timepiece that ticked out the seconds.'

The Imperial drawing-room

1871

Napoleon arrives

Napoleon lll arrives in Chislehurst

In early 1871 Mr. Lord, the stationmaster at Chislehurst, went to Camden Place with a message that a special train would depart in an hour's time to take the Empress to Dover to meet the exiled Emperor, who had been released. He arrived at Camden Place on 30 March and Queen Victoria again visited on the 3 April. The Queen's second visit set the tone and undoubtedly 'put Chislehurst on the map'. A succession of politicians and influential visitors brought prosperity to the area.

This was not simply a question of having celebrity tenants. The French court in exile now had a home in Chislehurst with the French flag flying and more and more court followers and sympathisers arriving, as they too fled the siege of Paris. Napoleon never abdicated and when he died at Camden Place in 1873, his death certificate recorded his occupation as *'Emperor of the French'*. He was their last Emperor.

Life at Chislehurst was very different from the grandeur to which the family was accustomed. Napoleon was an ill man but seems to have settled into English country life reasonably well: watching cricket at Bickley Park, Bromley and West Kent, walking to church on a Sunday and taking the train to London, travelling first class rather than accepting the offer of a special train. The local children loved him for the pennies he had in his pockets. The family's presence must have brought excitement as well as visitors and income to the area.

Life at Camden Place

The Prince Imperial's tutor provided and insight into life in exile.

'At five o'clock tea was served. We often forgot the time and talked on, sometimes until close to seven o'clock (the dinner hour) and then everyone fled in haste to dress as the gong in the corridor announced the first summons to dinner.

Dinner over, the men went into the smoking room and from there to billiards. The ladies settled themselves round the table in the large drawing room. The Comtesse Clary, Madame Lebreton and Mademoiselle de Larminat used to busy themselves with needlework. Dr Conneau and the Duc de Bassano played patience. Very often the Emperor would do the same or else he would sit and muse in a big armchair near the porcelain fireplace, wrapped in a cloud of cigarette smoke.

Whilst he lived, political factions were attracted to Kent. Supporters, politicians and royalty visited, whilst his enemies had spies based in the windmill at the top of Old Hill, watching and reporting on those visitors. Even after his death, there were those who pinned their hopes on the Prince Imperial becoming Napoleon IV. Callers to Camden Place included Queen Victoria, Prime Minister Gladstone and the Prince of Wales, who would later become Edward Vll. Victoria's youngest daughter Beatrice and the Prince Imperial became quite close.

The Emperor's death

The Emperor died at Camden Place on 9 January 1873, following a second operation to deal with his bladder stones. There were two French doctors in attendance, Conneau and Corvisart. The surgeon, Henry Thompson, was assisted by William Gull, Burdon Sanderson and John Foster. The anaesthetist was JT Clover.

An Imperial funeral

His death and funeral were huge events in Chislehurst. Twenty thousand mourners had filed past the coffin to pay their respects on the final Tuesday. The bells of St Nicholas' Anglican Church were tolled for the funeral itself.

The hearse was drawn by eight horses draped in black. The Prince Imperial walked behind followed by members of the Bonaparte family and representatives of the British and Italian Royal families. Only 200 could be squashed into St Mary's Catholic Church while many thousands stood outside.

The Napoleon bust

The sculptor Carpeaux arrived in England shortly before Napoleon lll. He had been the Prince Imperial's sculpture tutor and benefited from the benevolence of the Imperial family. Empress Eugénie and the Prince Imperial commissioned a portrait bust of Napoleon. Carpeaux began his work in 1872 but was interrupted by him having to suddenly return to France. He was summoned back to Chislehurst on Napoleon's death and completed the sculpture whilst Napoleon was lying in state. He stayed on at Camden Place for some three months.

Empress Eugénie and the Prince Imperial in mourning at Camden Place painted in 1874 by James Jacques Joseph Tissot. The Empress is in full mourning and the emblem of Bonapartism, the violets can be seen on the table.

The nine foot original can be seen at the Museum of Compiègne.

Chateau de Compiègne, Oise, France/Bridgeman Images

The Emperor died on Thursday the 9th inst., and by Saturday the little village of Chislehurst was filled to overflowing with an influx of persons drawn thither by motive either of curiosity, of sympathy or of respect. The inns and other places of accommodation were speedily filled, and many, who had intended to stay at Chislehurst till after the funeral, were obliged to return to London to sleep. The bulk of these immigrants were naturally Frenchmen.

The Graphic 25 January 1873

9th January
1873
Napoleon III dies

The Prince Imperial

For the fourteen-year old Prince Imperial moving to Chislehurst in 1870 must have been a huge change. He hardly spoke any English and settled in to his new environment slowly. But in the summer of 1872 it was suggested he should apply to be admitted as a Gentleman Cadet at the Royal Military Academy at Woolwich. It was a role he threw himself into and relished but would lead directly to his own untimely death. His father died the following year, leaving him as the only hope for reviving the Empire as Napoleon lV.

In 1874 the Prince Imperial turned eighteen. There were grand celebrations with marquees in the grounds of Camden Place and the Prince was feted in Chislehurst. Tom Bushell in *Imperial Chislehurst* describes the day:
'The railway station was gaily decorated and flew the tricolour of France, whilst in the main waiting room an inscription, wreathed in laurels and violets read 'Vive le Prince Imperial 16 mars, 1874' – and Chislehurst really meant it.'

The Prince Imperial's death

The Prince acquitted himself exceptionally well at Woolwich and graduated as an officer with top marks for practical gunnery. In his final exams in January 1875, he passed out seventh in the School and first in the final

exam. When his regiment was deployed to fight the Zulu War in 1879 the Prince was passionately keen to go with his comrades and despite his mother's objections, he obtained permission from Queen Victoria and the Duke of Cambridge, Commander-in-Chief of the British Army. The proviso was he went in the capacity of an observer.

One morning, the Prince Imperial's group went out scouting and were surprised by forty Zulu warriors. Tragically he and two others were killed in the skirmish. The next day his body was recovered and brought down from Zululand and returned to England on board the British troopship *HMS Orontes*, for burial in Chislehurst.

Breaking the news

The task of informing the Empress Eugénie that her only son had been killed, aged only 23, fell to John Robert Townshend, Lord Sydney. The Earl had been involved in organising the Royal visit to Paris and return visit of the Imperial family to Windsor in 1855. He regularly escorted Queen Victoria to her meetings with the Empress at Camden Place. At the time he was also Lord of the Manor at Chislehurst.

Lord Sydney

John Robert Townshend, born August 1805, became 3rd Viscount Sydney on his father's death in 1831 and was made an Earl in 1874. He was connected with the Court from an early age. He was successively Groom-in-Waiting to George IV, Lord-in-Waiting to William IV and held the same post with Queen Victoria. He was also Captain of the Yeomen of the Guard in the 1850s, Lord Chamberlain in the 1860s and '70s, and Lord Steward of the Queen's Household in the 1880s.

1879
Prince Imperial
is killed

This portrait of Earl Sydney hangs in Camden Place, on loan from the Chislehurst Society

The Prince returns to Chislehurst

The Prince Imperial's death in British uniform caused international news and comment. Tragically it meant that his mother faced organising a second funeral from Camden Place. Once again thousands came to pay their respects.

Memorials

Eugénie wanted to build a mausoleum in Chislehurst in order to provide a fitting resting place for her husband and son but did not succeed in getting the permissions needed. She remained at Camden Place until 1881 when she moved to Farnborough, Hampshire where she had St Michael's Abbey built as a memorial to her husband and son. In 1888 their bodies were moved from Chislehurst.

Chislehurst still remembers them, from the street names Prince Imperial Road, Empress

Photo by Stephanie Furquim Elias: Coopers School

Drive and Royal Parade to the two memorials in St. Mary's church and the Prince Imperial monument on the common, erected in 1881.

The large Celtic cross was designed by Edward Robson and paid for by the people of Chislehurst. On one side it is inscribed *'In memory of the Prince Imperial and in sorrow at his death, this cross is erected by the dwellers of Chislehurst 1880'* and on the other are words from the Prince's last will and testament.

1881
Empress Eugénie leaves

1888
Napoleon III and the Prince Imperial's bodies moved

Painting of Prince Imperial's funeral on display at Camden Place

The sale of Camden Place

After the Empress left Camden Place, which had been leased fully furnished to the Imperial family, Mr Strode and his family returned to Camden Place. They lived there until Strode's death in 1889 and were the final residents before Camden Place found a new purpose at the heart of Chislehurst Golf Club.

Everything went under the auctioneer's hammer even down to two rolls of oil cloth and two of linoleum from the kitchens.

Some high prices were obtained and the auction catalogue provides a record of the quality of the furnishings that the Imperial family had enjoyed.

Day 2 of the auction saw the furniture, room by room, go under the hammer. The billiard room had 13 items sold, fetching a total of £273, the equivalent of about £32,000 in 2018. Lot 221 was two large crimson damask window curtains with mahogany poles, rings and brackets selling for 18 shillings, a full-size billiard table with slate bed and oak frame earned £17.17s. Five sofas were sold and a massive library table of coloured buhl (elaborate inlaid work of tortoiseshell and brass on wood) with three drawers, richly mounted with masks, female busts and borders of chased ormolu, at 6 feet 5 inches long, went for £54 12s.

The valuable contents of Camden Place, Chislehurst

Comprising:

Fine old French and Flemish tapestries, old French furniture, decorative objects

Sevres, Dresden, Derby, Worcester and other porcelain.

Pictures, engravings and books; household furniture and the appointments of the bedrooms.

By order of the executors of Nathaniel W J. Strode esq. deceased, who let the Place furnished to the late Emperor Napoleon lll

for 11 years.

Will be sold by auction by Messers Christie, Manson and Woods

on the premises of Camden Place

Wednesday, June 12, 1889 and the two following days, at 1:00 PM precisely.

Viewing is allowed to those with a catalogue price one shilling each.

A future Club member makes a purchase

It appears that most of those bidding for items were men and are recorded in the auctioneer's annotated catalogue only by their surnames. However one lady was an active bidder on the first day. This was a Mrs. L. Jackson and it seems highly probable this was the same Mrs L. Jackson who became one of the early stars of ladies golf at Chislehurst. She bought a large dinner and dessert service of glazed ware with a band of coloured ornament on the border, consisting 17 oval dishes, 19 round dishes, 13 shell-shaped dishes, two pierced baskets and stands, soup tureen and cover and 115 plates, all for the price of £1.15s, over £220 at 2018 prices.

Art at Camden Place

Despite the sale of all the fixtures and fittings and changes over the years, there are still echoes of the former grandeur of Camden Place evident in the pillars and wood panelling, grand fireplaces and the murals.

The murals have been assessed and cleaned. Sotheby's in 1979 described the Oval Room paintings either side if the fireplace as 18th century *'Dutch School, a set of four wall panels, depicting canal and coastal scenes with elegant figures and rustics, oil on canvas'*.

According to Donald Sim, a Chislehurst member researched into their origin in 1920 and found the signature and date *'J. Janson 1780'*. He concluded that the artist was Johannes Janson, a Dutch painter and etcher, who was born in the East Indies in 1729 and taken to Holland by his parents. On viewing the paintings now no signature is visible. Sim put this down to the accumulation of dirt, but they have recently been cleaned and still no signature is evident!

There is little doubt that Strode installed the five oval scenes of landscapes and country houses that are in the main lounge because one of these is clearly the extended Camden Place. Sotheby's did not attribute this work to any particular artist or period. It is also believed that Strode installed the oval French painting above the main stairs depicting Leda and the Swan.

Only one article left in situ was likely to have been introduced by the Imperial family, which was the fireplace in the billiard room. It is an Egyptian porphyry fireplace, thought to have been given to Eugénie in 1869, at the opening of the Suez Canal.

The Eugénie bust

The bust of Eugénie, sculpted by Antony Samuel Adam-Solomon and dated 1863, was purchased and presented to the Club by Hubert Faber in 1936.

1889
The estate is bought
by William Willett

The developers

Only a few weeks after the furniture auction on 27 June 1889 the house and estate were sold by auction in London by Mr. David J. Chattell. The estate was 124 acres and included all of the land that would eventually become the properties and gardens on Camden Park Road and Wilderness Road.

The auctioneers identified the Camden Place estate as an opportunity for building speculation. They illustrated three possible development plans and detailed two schemes, one for 300 small cottage-size plots and the other divided the land into about 66 plots suitable for good quality detached housing. Both schemes involved a network of roads across the estate, connecting them with the existing public road to Bromley (now Old Hill).

As a consequence of this marketing effort it is not really surprising that Camden Place was bought by property developer, William Willett Snr.

The Willetts

The Willetts, father and son, were speculative builders of fine middle class houses in comfortable suburbs working with reputable architects, including Ernest Newton and Amos Faulkner.

The Willett business archives were lost in a bombing raid during the war so there are no documents recording the preferred plans, aspirations for the site or evidence indicating if building work ever began. Donald Sim thought it was probable. He pointed to the curious ridge in the valley that used to run across the

Willett and daylight saving

William Willett Jnr. is mainly remembered for the idea of daylight saving. It is said to have occurred to him in 1907, early one summer morning as he returned home from his customary canter over Chislehurst Common, when he noticed how many blinds were still down in the large houses that he passed.

present 11th and 14th holes towards the 13th green. He believed this represented the start of road construction or levelling operations or both and that this ridge was created using material excavated from what was originally a hillock, but as work progressed became the pit at the 13th hole. The pit was removed when the 13th hole was redesigned in 2003 and today there is little evidence of the ridge. Sim's theory is supported by the fact that this pit, unlike that at the 7th hole, is not shown on any of the old maps or any of the plans of the estate which accompanied the sale catalogue. It can therefore be assumed to have been dug after the purchase.

We know that after the purchase Willett Snr. took a back seat in plans relating to Camden Place and that his eldest son, William Willett Jnr. was the key player in all negotiations and decisions. The younger Willett built himself a house, The Cedars, opposite the entrance to Camden Place.

The William Willett Memorial in William Willett Wood

The role of the Conservators

The Chislehurst and St Pauls Cray Common Conservators were far from enthusiastic about this large green space in Chislehurst becoming a housing development and they stepped into the picture with significant impact.

They still controlled the 'ransom' strips of land that provided people with a right of way onto and off the Camden Park Estate. They contended that the rights of way only enabled Mr. Willett to use the approaches for the purpose of his personal enjoyment of Camden Place as a residence. Those rights could not be extended by him to allow that same right of way to any additional residences, or even for the delivery of building materials needed. Without the Conservators' support and consent the land could not be developed. Their contention brought the Willett plans to a halt.

The Conservators did not behave unreasonably, they only wanted to use their upper hand as a negotiating chip that would help them ensure a settlement that would benefit the parishioners and the community. In particular they wanted to preserve Weston's beautiful avenue of lime trees within Camden Park, extending along its eastern boundary.

Protracted negotiations took place between the Conservators, represented by the Chairman, Mr Travers Hawes, and Mr. Willett Jnr. Eventually they reached a agreement which was signed on the 18 April 1893.

The agreement

The agreement provided that if any building was undertaken within 400 feet of the boundary of Camden Park, then Mr. Willett or his successors would have to convey to the Conservators the strip of land on which the line of lime trees stood. This strip would be about 45 feet wide lying alongside the eastern boundary of the park. The Conservators would then move back the boundary fence so including the trees in the Common.

Until the avenue of trees was handed over to the Conservators (if ever) Mr Willett was only at liberty to cut down a third of them, provided that no two trees standing side by side were removed. This restriction would become subject to further negotiation later.

The agreement also specified that if Mr. Willett enlarged the private road leading from the southern entrance down the avenue to Camden Place, or created a new road along the strip of trees on the western side of the avenue, he would have to convey to the Conservators the site of the private road itself. The Conservators would then grant rights of use to any frontages.

This benefited the parishioners but considerably restricted the Willett development plans. As some compensation the negotiation granted enlargement of the Willetts' rights of way over the strips of the Common outside the southern and eastern entrances, allowing them to widen the roads across these strips.

No more preparations for building were carried out by Mr. Willett within the part of the park which is now the golf course.

The gate house is demolished

A supplement to this agreement was made between the Conservators and Willett signed on the 22 January 1894. This followed a decision, with the agreement of the Road Authority, to allow a considerable widening of the public roads which converge at the junction outside the entrance to Camden Place. The alterations to the roads involved the demolition of the large gate house inside the Camden Park gates and moving the gates and fencing further back down the avenue.

1893
Agreements reached

Thinking golf

Wholesale development of the Camden property for housing was now off the agenda but what else could the land be used for? From somewhere, the idea of a golf course came up as an option. There is no record of whose idea it was but the prime movers in the project were Mr. Alexander Travers Hawes and William Willett Jnr., the two who had been the main protagonists in the right of access negotiations. Although not overly interested in sport, Travers Hawes was keen to preserve as much of open space in Chislehurst as possible. William Willett, now living in the Cedars opposite to Camden Place, may have been attracted by the idea of having a golf club on his doorstep. Certainly golf was enjoying a huge boom in popularity making it a potentially attractive commercial opportunity. Bromley and Bickley Golf Club had successfully opened an 18-hole course in 1892. Golf was becoming big business. The planned Chislehurst Golf Club was to be owned and operated by William Willett Jnr. and golf may simply have been presented as a business proposition that appealed to him.

Whatever their motivations and despite any earlier differences, it seems these two men worked closely together in the formation of the Club. As the son of the estate owner and the family member responsible for it, William Willett undoubtedly held the whip hand. It would have been his final decision that Tom Dunn should be commissioned to design a 9-hole course and a very small ladies' course. It was agreed that Camden Place should be used as a temporary clubhouse and that Mr Willett should run the club, assisted by a committee and the necessary staff. In 1893 Camden Place was an empty building, unchanged since the days of the Imperial family. Some redecoration and internal alterations were necessary for it to serve its new function. The catering area was expanded, changing facilities created and a room for a Club Professional added. The building was then ready for its new use.

Changes since 1894

Since becoming a clubhouse in 1894 the property has undergone a few changes necessary to satisfy the functional and evolving needs of a successful golf club and to maintain the fabric of a Grade ll* listed building.

The most obvious structural change was the replacement of the old glass conservatory, built by Nathaniel Strode. In the early golf club days this room was popular with the ladies who used it for tea but it had to be demolished when it was deemed beyond repair. The brick Faber lounge, a most generous gift to the Club from Hubert Faber in 1938, was not without its critics as some were unhappy that the design was unsympathetic to the rest of the building. As a result it was initially underused, since it was sparsely furnished and lacked any real purpose.

In the 60s a temporary bar was set up and the Faber lounge was later transformed into the spike bar, allowing members to have a drink without the necessity of changing from golfing attire.

Hubert Faber and the Faber Lounge

H. L. Faber joined the Board in 1934. He lived at Beechcroft in Camden Park Road. He was a widower and when his daughter left home in 1936, he moved into a suite of four rooms above the mixed lounge. He called this the Empress Suite and added, at considerable expense, a bathroom and other facilities. He was a generous benefactor to the Club also providing practical equipment including a water softener and a refrigerator and of course the beautiful marble bust of the Empress Eugénie.

The aftermath of war

Camden Place did not escape unscathed from World War II. Besides smashed windows and unexploded bombs it was hit directly by an incendiary bomb and suffered considerable damage from both the fire and water used to tackle it.

Even after the war the dry rot, resulting from the bomb damage, continued to appear. In 1946 the fungus appeared in the dining-room. Urgent action was needed and the directors decided on a bold move, given the seriousness of the Company finances. They chose to combine the work to deal with the war damage alongside substantial alterations to the interior.

These improvements involved the remodelling of the changing rooms for both men and women, whilst also improving the kitchen area and wine and liquor stores on the ground floor. On the upper floor there was redesigning and partitioning of some of the rooms to provide increased residential accommodation, consisting of four flats and twelve rooms along with improved staff quarters. The total cost, including restoration of the war damage and the treatment of the dry rot, was almost £40,000, of which £28,000 was paid by the War Damage Commission and £6,000 was loaned by some members of the golf club. The balance was obtained on mortgage.

Unfortunately post-war rebuilding and the settlement of war damage claims took so long that the work was not completed until

1951. But the dry rot problem was to become a wartime legacy with another extensive outbreak of damage to the ceiling of the billiard room being discovered in 1978 and necessitating more costly repairs.

Saving the Temple

By 1954 the Temple was looking decidedly ramshackle and T. Brammall Daniel offered to contribute the cost of its restoration. In 1959 Brigadier Pocock made a similar offer. The Board was not receptive as repairs might cost £1,000 and the Temple was in no danger of complete collapse. It continued to look ramshackle.

In *Golf Illustrated* 1934 'Brer Rabbit concluded a complimentary article about the course with the thought that *'as a clubhouse (Camden Place) has probably been detested and damned by every secretary responsible for its maintenance.'*

46

Should we sell?

Camden Place is a Grade ll* listed building. Its age and historic interest means any changes and upkeep need permission. Maintaining such a building is expensive and perhaps it is not surprising that over the years there have been thoughts of selling it and creating a purpose-built clubhouse elsewhere on the grounds.

As late as 1968 negotiations took place with the Mutual Householders Association looking to create homes for the retired elderly. The directors of Camden Place Ltd. and the Committee of the Golf Club were in favour of the proposals in principle because the scheme offered a number of benefits. It would rid the Company of the ever-increasing cost of repairs and maintenance of an aging listed building and remove the challenges of managing residential accommodation. At the same time it could generate a substantial sum of money towards a brand new purpose-built clubhouse. The negotiations advanced during the course of the year and it appeared that the sale was likely to go ahead but the Association suddenly and unexpectedly announced that they would not proceed with the purchase.

Despite a few other shows of interest from one of two similar organisations, nothing of significance materialised and over time the golf club members decided the Camden Place was not so bad after all and they would prefer to keep it.

It seems that the Club's forward-thinking directors made a sensible precautionary move in 1950. They made a formal application, on behalf of Camden Place Ltd. for an assessment of how much compensation would be payable if, in the future, they were refused planning permission to develop properties on the golf course.

The amount of potential compensation was agreed and valued in 1953 at £13,100. The directors were advised not to make an immediate application for planning permission, so the agreed sum had not been paid.

By 1968 the position on land usage locally was much clearer because the West Kent Development Plan had identified Camden Place as an open space; a golf course, not open to the public. The Company was advised that planning permission would not be granted for the development of any part of the course.

The Directors considered it to be their duty, in the interests of the company, to submit an application for planning permission to build houses on the golf course. As expected, permission was refused and as a consequence, the Company claimed payment of the agreed compensation. The amount paid out was increased to £14,217, a little more than the 1953 valuation because some interest was added.

Improving the clubhouse

Once the decision not to sell was made, it was felt that the time was right to make substantial alterations to the ground floor, in order to provide better facilities for club members. In 1969 it was decided to undertake a number of significant improvements.

The first was to switch the location of the Members' Bar (then the Men's Bar) and the club office, moving the bar from the front of the building to its present location and making an opening through the northern wall of the mixed lounge, installing a bar to serve both the lounge and the newly relocated Men's Bar. New access to the billiard room was opened up.

A new central heating system was installed, improved catering facilities provided and the men's and ladies' changing rooms and toilet facilities modernised and expanded. Outside a modern professional's shop and a trolley shed were constructed.

The consent of the GLC Historic Buildings Committee had to be obtained for some of the alterations. The work was completed in 1971 and the results were widely appreciated. The Mixed Lounge, which had been seldom used, was now much more popular and the newly located Men's Bar had views over the course.

Paying the bill

The cost of all these alterations and some redecoration was about £32,500. To pay for this about £12,500 was raised by compulsory interest free loans from all the members of the club, proportional to the annual subscriptions.

Some £7,500 was borrowed from the bank and the balance came out of the sum of £14,217 received in 1970 as compensation under the Town and Country planning legislation for the loss of development rights in respect of the golf course.

Both Camden and then Bonar worked on their development plans with the architects George Dance. Lord Camden's work almost certainly was started by George Dance the elder (1695-1768) and his son George Dance the Younger (1741-1825) probably saw its completion This seems likely because by the time of his father's death, the younger had already joined the family firm. It is unlikely that he had begun the work on the Camden commission as he spent the six years between 1759 - 1765 studying architecture and draughtsmanship in Rome. We do know that it was Dance the younger whom Thomson Bonar turned to for the second stage of developing Camden Place.

Camden Place in 1780

By the time Lord Camden had finished changing Weston's L shaped house it had two entrance halls and the magnificent drawing room.

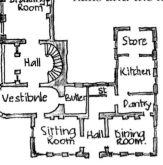

The house in 1807

The house after Thompson Bonar's extensions. By closing off the entrance and moving the stairs he gave his new library the distinctive shape of the Oval Room. His layout meant the kitchen and dining room were at opposite ends of the building.

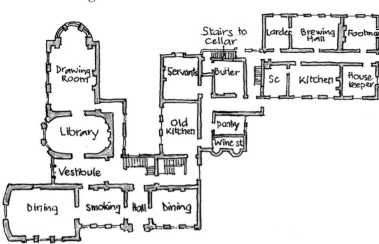

The Strode house at 1870

The extent of Strode's changes is evident, The Oval Room has become a drawing room, there is a new glass conservatory and a picture gallery has been created in the centre of the building, billiards has its own room and there is a library and study overlooking the rear of the property.

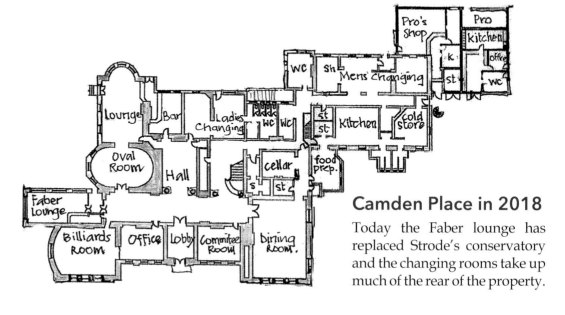

Camden Place in 2018

Today the Faber lounge has replaced Strode's conservatory and the changing rooms take up much of the rear of the property.

The floor plans of Camden Place through the years were produced for us by club member Bob Mathews.

Ongoing challenge

Maintaining the fabric of Camden Place remains a constant and expensive challenge. But there have been a few developments over and above the general maintenance worthy of note.

1977 was the Queen's Jubilee Year. Ian Todman (Captain 1976) championed the idea of a new Jubilee Terrace. The Board were reluctant but Ian worked hard to get the members to pledge financial support. Eventually the Board agreed and levied an additional £6 from every member to fund the cost. The Jubilee Terrace was inaugurated with a barbeque party and was ready in time for the official celebrations. Views across the course and beautiful sunsets have been appreciated ever since.

Funding projects

The policy of the Club from the outset had been not to create financial surpluses and indeed it was a stated policy after the war that subscriptions should effectively only cover operational costs. There was no sense that a sinking fund would be prudent or that capital projects would become essential and require funding.

This started to change under Peter Gibson's chairmanship and was certainly no constraint to the Board headed by Michael Hollingsworth from 1998. We had secured a VAT rebate of £104,269 in 1995 and a sub committee concluded that it should be spent externally on a new sprinkler system (£85,000) and the balance on rewiring the clubhouse and its security systems. The rewiring turned into a

major exercise costing over £130,000.

Meanwhile plans were drawn up for extensive rebuilding of the machinery sheds. The drivers of this project were David Spragg (Captain 1998) and Graham Wake, Property Director. Somehow during this process Bromley Council announced it had been unaware of the residents at Camden Place. As a result some additional works were needed to satisfy fire regulations. The eventual overall cost of all works was £260,000, some of which was funded by a local authority grant of £48,000 and an interest free loan from the R&A provided another £30,000.

Club Captain L. Rigden and Ian Todman at the opening of Jubilee Terrace

More recent works

A number of improvements have been undertaken.

- Both locker rooms were upgraded, the men's facilities being completed in 2005 (£62,000) and the ladies' locker room was renovated in 2012 (£79,000).

- A disabled toilet and disabled access to Jubilee Terrace were both added in 2006.

- The Mixed Lounge was redecorated and the murals cleaned and rearranged between 2006 and 2008.

- The redecoration of the hall and stairway was the most extensive and expensive programme carried out by the Club in some years. It was completed in 2013 at a cost of close to £100,000. The style was in keeping with the age and historical nature of the building, with patterned carpeting and large light-fittings.

- The Billiard room was refurbished soon afterwards and the external painting of the clubhouse, along with the repair and refurbishment of the main roof was also completed.

- At the start of 2014 and immediately after his investiture as Captain, Philip Matthews gathered together a happy band of assistants, DIY-ers and a motley selection of others and redecorated and refurbished the Faber Bar. Only limited funds were made available by the Board and self-help was the only real option.

In 2017, splendid new gates were finally installed at the southern entrance after a gap of 74 years. Camden Place once more gives a striking first impression made possible to a large extent by an interest free loan from a member.

Contents

2

Creating
a Golf
Club

Chislehurst Golf Club began as a proprietors' club boasting just 9 holes but was quickly
bought by members and lengthened to 18 holes – eventually becoming a members' club.
This section traces some of the key developments and changes from the Club's opening in
1894 and highlights some of the people responsible for shaping and developing the short

Designing the course

A golf club needs more than a clubhouse, no matter how impressive its heritage. Once the idea for a golf club on Camden Park had taken root, the next step was to design a course.

In 1893 Tom Dunn was invited to design a 9-hole parkland course and a separate, very short ladies' course. Just like the house, the course would evolve over time, not simply changing as the surrounding landscape matured, but as the result of several significant modifications and developments.

Dunn's services as a course architect were in demand. In the space of ten years the number of courses in England grew from 481 to 1,571, Chislehurst was just one of the 137 courses Dunn designed before his death at just 52 years of age.

Tom Dunn

Tom Dunn (1850-1902)

Tom Dunn grew up in a golfing family. His father, William Dunn Sr., was the greenkeeper at Blackheath until 1864 and taught his son all aspects of the business of golf, including club manufacture and groundsmanship.

A good golfer, Tom Dunn competed in the Open Championship eight times but never improved on the sixth place he achieved at his first attempt in 1868. He first became a professional in North Berwick and then moved to the London Scottish Golf Club at Wimbledon.

In 1889 he was appointed greenkeeper and club maker to the Tooting Bec Golf Club, where he laid out the Furzedown course. This was note-worthy because it was the first course near London to be laid out in a park, attached to a private mansion. Camden Place would be another such site.

In the *Illustrated Sporting and Dramatic News 28 July 1894* the following comments were made *'...Tom Dunn has had enormous practice in this particular kind of work and is certain to make the most of any ground entrusted to his care. At Chislehurst it seems to me he has been surprisingly successful and whilst every available hazard has been utilised to the full, the course is free from that great bane of 9-hole courses, crossing'.*

No detailed plans of Dunn's 9-hole layout have survived. Some idea of what the course was like can be gleaned from descriptions that were given in Golf and the 1894 Golf Annual.

The description of how the course may have been laid out is based on what is known about the location of tees, fairways and greens but it is not a complete picture. Analysis of these has led to suggestions for alternative locations for holes 6 – 9 from the layout described in Bill Mitchell's centenary book; neither is necessarily right, both are just informed speculation.

The ladies' course

There are no details of the ladies course. We know it was also designed by Dunn, it was tiny and sited on flat ground adjacent to Camden Place. It only existed for five or six years, until it was incorporated into the extended 18-hole course.

1894
Dunn designs
9 hole course

*View from the current 7th green
back across 1st green*

Hole No. 1
377 yards

The 1st tee is near the clubhouse. An artificial bunker about 100 yards off has to be cleared with the drive. That accomplished, a longish and very ticklish approach shot has to be played, the green being on a flat at the base of the considerable slope with very penal consequences, because of a ditch immediately beyond in the case of too strong a shot.

Tee
Middle of the present 18th fairway, some yards forward from the present ladies tee at the 1st hole.

Fairway
Across the humps on 18th forward of 18th tee, then right of the pond on 1st fairway, down to green.

Green
A built up flat area on the extreme left of the present first fairway, approximately level with half way along the length of the old sand quarry at the present 7th hole.

Hole No.2
477 yards

The 2nd hole is the longest of the nine. An artificial bunker of considerable height has to be cleared with the drive and then with clean straight play the green may be reached with a good brassy shot and an iron approach. There are difficulties in the way, in the shape of a filled up ditch and a fairly thick hawthorn hedge. A sliced ball for the second shot means practically a lost hole. The green, which is in an angle at a slight eminence, requires very careful manipulation, because of the boundary hazards.

Tee
In what is now the rough on the right hand side of the 1st fairway, above the bunkers to the right of the present 6th green.

Fairway
Up the present 6th fairway, through the present 6th and 3rd tees to the far side of the present 4th fairway.

Green
Left hand side of the present 4th fairway, on the flat area about level with current back tee at 3rd.

Hole No.9
260 yards

The distance to the home hole is 260 yard. There is a pond on the left. The course is practically open, though a decided slope has to be guarded against in regards to carry and run of the drive. A strongish iron shot for a second ought to reach the green and the hole ought to be taken easily enough in 4.

Tee
Somewhere just above the current 15th green.

Fairway
Along the flat above the 15th fairway and using the left side of the 14th hole.

Green
Between the practice green and the humps on current 15th hole.

Hole No.8
261 yards

The distance to the 8th hole is 261 yards, the course being almost directly downwards again. A good drive leaves a fairly short approach requiring however, discrimination, as the green is once again on the slope.

Tee
Possibly somewhere behind the current 10th green, aiming over the existing back tee on 11th hole.

Fairway
Mainly the current 11th hole.

Green
Probably on the crossover between current 8th and 11th holes.

Hole No.3
317 yards

The 3rd hole is right back side by side with the course to the 2nd but is considerably shorter. The same natural difficulties have to be encountered with the addition of an artificial bunker guarding the green. A decent drive and brassy shot for second ought to carry the green.

Tee
Centre of the present 4th fairway, aiming to the right of current 2nd green.

Fairway
Across the present 4th and 3rd fairways and back down the present 2nd fairway.

Green
Near the grass bunker on the present 2nd fairway, some 120 yards from the tee..

Hole No.4
150 yards

The 4th hole is a club drive without any obstacle, unless of course, there is crooked play, with rough either side.

Tee
Near the grass bunker on the present 2nd fairway.

Fairway
Back down the present 2nd fairway and across what is now 6th green.

Green
Present 1st green.

Hole No.5
117 yards

The 5th hole is the most picturesque of the nine. The tee for it is low down in Seven Oaks Valley and though the span from there to the hole is only 117 yards, a yawning quarry has to be cleared with an uphill drive, the green being just on the higher side of this morally depressing obstacle. It is a hole for two or three at the most with decent play.

Tee
Present ladies tee at the 7th, maybe a few yards further back.

Fairway
None, just over the quarry.

Green
Present seventh green, close to the edge of the quarry.

Hole No.7
228 yards

Next to the 5th hole the seventh is the most sporting of the course. The tee has, to the left, an aggravation of the valley or ravine which has to be crossed on going to the sixth; it is, moreover faced by a set of thick grown hawthorn trees, while on either side a pulled or sliced ball is doomed. In order to do justice to this hole a clear drive is indispensable. A fairly long approaches is then all that is required to reach the green, which with a distance of 228 yards lies at the top of the slope.

Tee
Possibly close to but in front of the forward men's 14th tee.

Fairway
Possibly up the right hand half of the current 14th fairway.

Green
Possibly on right of current 14th fairway, near the grass bunker.

Hole No.6
unknown

Going to the 6th, the tee is placed on the hither side of a deep valley or slope and a clean straight drive is necessary in order to avoid first of all the dangers of the hollow, where bad ground abounds, and the thick trees to the right. A good drive, however will leave an easy iron approach, though great care is required in that latter operation, the green being on a slope.

Tee
Probably in the wood to the right rear of the present 7th green.

Fairway
Across the valley to top of current 11th, to right of oak tree.

Green
Possibly on the lower slope of the current 11th fairway, short and right of the current green.

Attracting members

CGC now had a clubhouse and two courses which were ready to play by April 1894. All that was needed now was people to enjoy it. One of the first mentions of the Club can be found in an advertisement for members placed in *Golf* on 27 April 1894 by the new Club's President, the Right Hon. Lord Walter Gordon Lennox M.P. In it he describes the courses and clubhouse, announces that the formal opening would be in early May 1894 and invites applications for particulars.

This first membership marketing campaign seems to have been successful. By the time of the official opening, *'the membership of the Club already exceeded 100'* according to a report in Golf 24 July 1894. There was an annual subscription fee of six guineas for men and three guineas for ladies and the Club was about to introduce an entrance fee.

From the outset Chislehurst was a family club. This was ensured by the simultaneous creation of the ladies' course and the provision of a ladies' club-room overlooking the action. The co-existence of a croquet lawn, a tennis pavilion with one gravel court and six lawn tennis courts, alongside the opportunity for squash, billiards (popular then with ladies and men), dance classes and bridge meant there was a range of pastimes and activities available. There really was something for all the family.

April
1894
CGC advertises
for members

No play was allowed on Sundays.

According to an article in the **Dundee Evening Telegraph** of 22 October 1895, it seems that Chislehurst was unusual in its approach to Sunday golf. In most other private clubs, golf on Sunday was as common as golf on Saturday. Proprietor William Willett would not allow Sunday golf, even though it probably cost him potential revenue.

Inauguration of the Club

O n Saturday 26 May 1894 Chislehurst Golf Club was formally inaugurated. At that first meeting of members a provisional committee was established consisting of the President, Lord Walter Gordon Lennox, a Vice President, Sir Pattison Nickalls J.P and the Hon. Secretary Mr Ernest Satow-Allen. The first Captain was John Dun and other members of the committee included the architects of the Club, Mr Travers Hawes and William Willett Jnr. The Club appointed Mr Dan Bryson as Professional.

Saturday 26 May

1894

CGC is formally inaugurated

Peter Skinner (Captain 2013) being helped into his jacket by Senior Past Captain Dr Ian Kelsey Fry (Captain 1969).

John Dun

John Dun had been Captain of Royal Liverpool at Hoylake in 1873 and 1874. Dun insisted that he wear his Hoylake captain's red coat with the dark green collar at Chislehurst. It is thought that Hoylake's close connection with the Liverpool Hunt Club influenced their choice of jacket.

So the Hoylake tradition was shared and took root at CGC. A replica of Dun's coat has been worn by all subsequent Chislehurst Club Captains. Since the 1970s the new captain has received his red jacket during the Annual Men's Dinner.

The portrait of Jon Dun was presented to the Club by Mr Leonard R Powell at the Annual Dinner in 1895. The portrait was painted by Rudolf Blind (1846-1889) and must therefore have been painted during Dun's days at Hoylake.

21 July

1894

CGC is formally
opened

The formal opening

Camden Place was redecorated and the two courses were ready for play by the members from about mid-June but the formal opening of the club took place on 21 July 1894.

The opening ceremony was performed by the Right Hon. A.J. Balfour M.P. who was at the time Captain of the Royal and Ancient Golf Club and Conservative Leader in the House of Commons. (In 1902 he was to become Prime Minister and later Earl Balfour). Balfour was much in demand as an opener of golf clubs and he had a particular connection to Chislehurst because his golf teacher was the course designer Tom Dunn.

Mr Balfour and his brother Mr G. W. Balfour M.P. travelled from London to Chislehurst for the opening in a special train, placed at his disposal by the South Eastern Railway Company. They were met at the station by Mr. Travers Hawes.

The formal proceedings began with a luncheon for 120, served in the impressive wood-panelled dining room. There were a number of distinguished guests present. According to the *Bromley Chronicle 'the luncheon was of the most recherché character, having been ably prepared by Mr and Mrs Pilcher, the steward and stewardess of the club'*.

In his speech Arthur Balfour described golf as, *'The most difficult game perhaps that exists'* and had a warning for novices to the game *'It is very easy in the early period of golfing education to acquire tricks and faults which will forever prevent that player reaching the higher excellences of the game'*.

A.J. Balfour putting

'You have undoubtedly, it must be evident to everyone who hears me, the best golf clubhouse in existence. I do not suppose that any other club, however ancient or famous, however large the number of its members, has ever been housed in a palace before.'

A.J. Balfour at the lunch to formally open Chislehurst Golf Club.

Members buy the Club: 1899

The club flourished from its opening in 1894 but its long-term future was not assured. It was a proprietary club, with the land still owned by William Willett Snr. and the Club operated by his son. A very real danger was that the Willetts, or their successors, might in the future choose to close the Club in order to build on the land.

In about 1897 Alexander Travers Hawes came up with a scheme to address this risk head on and ensure the continuation of the Club, so preserving the golf courses from future builders and ensuring this corner of Chislehurst remained green. He proposed forming a limited company which would purchase both Camden Place and the two golf courses from William Willett Snr. and buy out the proprietary interest in the golf club from Willett Jnr.

Camden Place sale agreed

The Willetts agreed to the sale in principle for a price of £36,000 but they wanted it to be subject to certain conditions. These included changes to the restrictions relating to their access across the Common. The negotiations for the sale would therefore involve not just the Club but also the Commons Conservators where Mr. Travers Hawes was Chairman.

Although happy to sell Camden Place and the golf course, the Willetts planned to retain the part of the estate called the Wilderness (now Wilderness Road) for building purposes. They wanted to ensure that there were two main means of access for this development from the public road because, if Camden Place were sold, there would be no access to the Wilderness through the southern entrance gates. This would leave only the original eastern entrance to the estate as a means of access to the Wilderness.

Mr. Willett Snr. stipulated that the sale of Camden Place should be conditional upon the Commons Conservators granting him the right to construct another access road from Prince Imperial Road, across the Common to the Wilderness. He also wanted certain other modifications to the agreement made between himself and the Conservators on the 18 April 1893.

It is not hard to imagine that the Willetts' requests caused the Conservators some deliberation and presumably at times it was slightly awkward for Mr Travers Hawes who was wearing his two different hats, Chairman of the Conservators and champion of the embryonic Camden Place Ltd. It seems the Conservators were persuaded by the fact that the proposals put forward were, to all intents and purposes, supported by the large number of club members and residents who were about to lend a substantial sum of money to the Golf Club project. The fact that this scheme also prevented any further building on a large part of the Camden Park estate must have been an important consideration. Eventually an arrangement was arrived at and embodied in a new agreement between Mr Willett and the Conservators dated the 21 February 1899.

Camden Place Ltd is incorporated

At the same time as these negotiations were taking place, Mr Travers Hawes set about forming a company and borrowing the necessary £36,000. The company was named Camden Place Limited and it was incorporated on the 5 August 1898 with a nominal capital of £78, divided into 1560 shares of one shilling each.

The main purpose of the company was to acquire Camden Place and the associated land and to promote and run a golf club. There was a power to issue debentures, charged against the company's property.

In 1898 £36,000 was a very large sum of money (equivalent to about £4.5 million in 2018) but the persuasive Mr Travers Hawes personally solicited contributions from the members of the Golf Club, their friends and neighbours and the local residents. There were many who, like him, were anxious that Camden Park should remain an open space. There were contributions from £50 to £2,000. The contributors were to receive debentures issued by the Company. There was a slight hiccup when the target had nearly been reached and one or two people withdrew. William Willett Jnr., who had already contributed £3,000, saved the day by coming forward with another £2,000.

5 August
1898
Camden Place Ltd
is incorporated

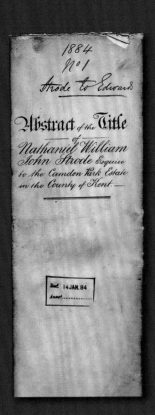

1884
No 1
Strode to Edwards

Abstract of the Title
of
Nathaniel William
John Strode Esquire
to the Camden Park Estate
in the County of Kent.

Recd 14 JAN. 84
Answr ....

CAMDEN PLACE,
LIMITED.

ISSUE of £36,000 FIRST MORTGAGE DEBENTURES, carrying Interest
at the rate of 2½ per cent. per annum.

First Mortgage Debenture.

£100   No. 174

CAMDEN PLACE, LIMITED (hereinafter called the Company), will, on the 1st day of July, 1911, or on such earlier date as the principal moneys hereby secured shall become payable, in accordance with the Conditions endorsed hereon, pay to Robert Whyse of Oakwood Chislehurst or other the registered holder of this Debenture, his executors or administrators, the sum of £100.

AND the Company will, until payment of the principal moneys hereby secured, pay to the registered holder hereof, his executors or administrators, interest on the said sum of £100, at the rate of Two-and-a-half per cent. per annum, by half-yearly payments on the 1st day of January and the 1st day of July, the first apportioned payment to be made on the 1st day of January, 1900.

AND the Company hereby charges with such payments its goods, book debts, chattels, effects, real and personal property, assets, business, goodwill and undertaking both present and future, not respectively charged by the Trust Deed mentioned below.

THE holders of the Debentures of this issue are and will be entitled to the benefit of and subject to the provisions contained in a Trust Deed, dated the 17th day of July, 1899, and made between the Company of the one part, and SIR PATTESON NICKALLS, JOHN DUN and ALEXANDER TRAVERS HAWES of the other part.

THIS Debenture is issued upon and subject to the Conditions endorsed hereon, which shall be read as part of this Debenture, and which the Company covenants to observe and perform in every respect.

GIVEN under the Common Seal of the Company, this Seventeenth day of July, 1899.

John Dun
A. Travers Hawes   } Directors.

Thomas Gilroy   Secretary.

Roberts & Leete Ltd. Printers, London.

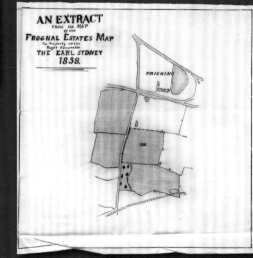

1884.
No 2
Strode to Edwards

Supplemental
Abstract of Title
to
Freehold Hereditaments
part of the Camden Park
Estate Kent.

Recd 15 MAR. 84
Answr ....

AN EXTRACT
from a Plan of
The Estate of
Charles Townshend Esqr
in Chisleburst, Mottingham & Bromley
in the County of Kent
(heretofore the Property of
Thomas Faringdon Esqr deceased.)
1781.

Name of Pieces	Contents	Tenants
22	Black Lands	1 3 16	Wm. Baker
23	Ditto	3 1 19	do
24	Ditto	3 1 13	do
25	Ditto	2 2 31	do

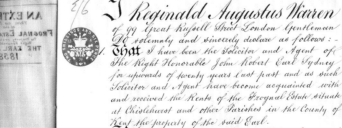

3/6

I Reginald Augustus Warren
of 99 Great Russell Street London Gentleman
Do solemnly and sincerely declare as follows:-
1. That I have been the Solicitor and Agent of
The Right Honorable John Robert Earl Sydney
for upwards of twenty years last past and as such
Solicitor and Agent have become acquainted with
and received the Rents of the Frognal Estate situate
at Chislehurst and other Parishes in the County of
Kent the property of the said Earl.
2. That I know the piece of land containing four acres two
roods and eight perches or thereabouts being the field No 125
on the Frognal Estate Plan 1858 (a tracing from which Plan
is hereto annexed) situate at Prickend Chislehurst aforesaid
now occupied by Mr Wood and Son on a yearly Tenancy
expiring at Michaelmas next and contracted to be sold by
the said Earl to Owen Edwards of Camden Wood Chislehurst
aforesaid Gentleman and say that the said Earl for a period
of twenty years last past has received the rent or enjoyed
the uninterrupted possession of the said piece of land.
3. That from a perusal of a Plan and particulars of the Estate
of Charles Townshend Esquire (a Great Uncle of the said Earl)

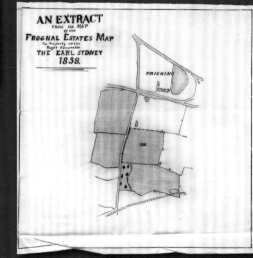

AN EXTRACT
FROM the MAP
of the
FROGNAL ESTATES MAP
The Property of the
Right Honorable
THE EARL SYDNEY
1858.

PRICKING

126

8 May
1899
Camden Place Ltd
purchases
the golf course

17 July
1899
Trust deed signed
securing the debentures
for the Company

The deal is signed

Once agreement with the Conservators had been reached Mr. Willett Snr. and Camden Place Limited agreed terms for the sale and purchase of Camden Place and the golf course on the 27 February 1899. This agreement also included the Company taking on the proprietary interests of Mr. Willett Jnr. in the running of the Golf Club. The conveyance of the property was dated the 8 May 1899.

The last step in the Travers Hawes scheme was the issuing of debentures to those who had contributed to raising the purchase price. The Company's Articles of Association only allowed the directors to raise up to £39,000 by the issue of debentures and accordingly they issued the first mortgage debentures for £35,900. Presumably £100 was not forthcoming at the last minute. A second mortgage debenture was issued for £ 3,000 all of which was taken up by William Willett Snr.

All the debentures were secured by means of a trust deed, dated the 17 July 1899, on the freehold of Camden Place and the golf course land. The debentures carried interest at the rate of 2½% per annum. The principal of the sums of money secured was to be repaid on the 1 July 1911. Under this trust deed the debentures did not become repayable before 1911, even if the Company defaulted in the payment of interest.

The Travers Hawes' solution meant that the directors of the Company were obliged to conduct its business in the interest of the debenture holders. The Articles of Association provided that each share carried one vote at a general meeting but only if the shareholder also held £25 of debentures against that share. There was therefore no conflict of interest because the shareholders and the debenture holders were the same individuals, each holding shares in proportion to debentures, namely one shilling share for each £25 of debenture.

Alexander Travers Hawes' efforts meant that the existence of the Golf Club was safeguarded, at least until 1911. But it was appreciated, even at this early stage, that if the Club was to survive after that date some further financial arrangements would be needed.

Post-purchase celebrations

On Saturday, 24 June 1899 another luncheon for 120 was held at Camden Place, this time to celebrate the purchase of the club.

The first captain John Dun was now Chairman of Camden Place Ltd. In his speech he paid tribute to the great exertions of Mr Travers Hawes in bringing the purchase scheme to fruition. Praising Mr Travers Hawes' energy, perseverance and tact in overcoming the many obstacles involved, he presented him with a handsome silver bowl as a testimony to the esteem and thanks of members and friends.

After the lunch, two foursomes were played. The scene was described in Golf Illustrated in the following words: *'The lovely park, with its gracefully undulating scenery, was looking at its best, and the presence of a large number of fair women in brave attire and bronzed golfers in scarlet coats, added a charm which the imagination can faintly picture.'* In the first match Mr Gerald Balfour and Mr John Penn beat Mr A.J. Balfour and Mr D. Blyth by 8 and 6 and in the second W.C. Gully (Speaker of the House of Commons) and A. Graham Murray (Lord Advocate) halved with Sir John Lubbock and Sir Samuel Hoare. Clearly enjoying the game Mr. A. J. Balfour's foursome played a few more holes but they had to leave to catch the 6.01 pm train to Charing Cross, to which a saloon carriage was specially attached. A more modest transport arrangement than the special train laid on for them when the Club was first opened in 1894.

Travers Hawes Bowl

In 1934 the bowl was brought back and presented to the golf club by Travers Hawes' widow. Known as the Travers Hawes Bowl it was one of the Club's most treasured trophies, played for annually. Unfortunately it was stolen in 1983.

From 9 to 18 holes:1900

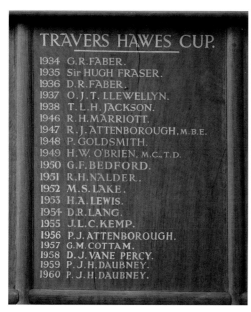

TRAVERS HAWES CUP.

1934 G.R.FABER.
1935 Sir HUGH FRASER.
1936 D.R.FABER.
1937 O.J.T.LLEWELLYN.
1938 T.L.H.JACKSON.
1946 R.H.MARRIOTT.
1947 R.J.ATTENBOROUGH, M.B.E.
1948 P.GOLDSMITH.
1949 H.W.O'BRIEN, M.C.,T.D.
1950 G.F.BEDFORD.
1951 R.H.NALDER.
1952 M.S.LAKE.
1953 H.A.LEWIS.
1954 D.R.LANG.
1955 J.L.C.KEMP.
1956 P.J.ATTENBOROUGH.
1957 G.M.COTTAM.
1958 D.J.VANE PERCY.
1959 P.J.H.DAUBNEY.
1960 P.J.H.DAUBNEY.

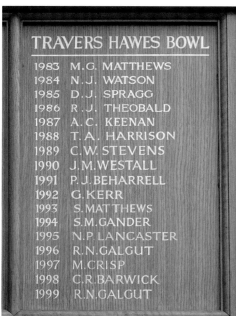

TRAVERS HAWES BOWL

1983 M.G.MATTHEWS
1984 N.J.WATSON
1985 D.J.SPRAGG
1986 R.J.THEOBALD
1987 A.C.KEENAN
1988 T.A.HARRISON
1989 C.W.STEVENS
1990 J.M.WESTALL
1991 P.J.BEHARRELL
1992 G.KERR
1993 S.MATTHEWS
1994 S.M.GANDER
1995 N.P.LANCASTER
1996 R.N.GALGUT
1997 M.CRISP
1998 C.R.BARWICK
1999 R.N.GALGUT

The Travers Hawes Cup was one of the Club's oldest competitions renamed the Travers Hawes Bowl in 1934

Since the Club's foundation in 1894 it had been the ambition of the members to expand the course to 18 holes. Whilst Mr Willett remained sole proprietor there was still the threat of potential building development so this had not been sensible. Once Camden Place Ltd. had taken ownership the members' vision was quickly to become a reality.

Only 63 ½ acres had been sold to the Company and that included the footprint of Camden Place itself. This was inadequate for 18 holes and it was therefore necessary to acquire more land. Fortunately the Club was able to obtain leases for another four acres. This comprised of a small field around the site of the present 4th green and a piece of land located between Willow Grove and an imaginary straight line running across the present third and fourth holes, approximately along the line of the ditch which crosses the third hole. This included the 1¼ acre site which would be given over to allotments during WWI and sub-let to Chislehurst and Sidcup Urban District Council in October 1920. Although subsequently sold it is still allotments today.

Mr Easton Devonshire

Designing the new course was undertaken by a club member, Mr Easton Devonshire. It does not seem he had any previous experience in designing golf courses but he was one of the most ardent advocates for the course extension and he tackled the task with enthusiasm. The legendary course designer Harry S. Colt added his signature to Devonshire's design and Chislehurst is attributed to him by the Colt Association, but the extent of his influence is unknown. The practical work of extending the course was supervised by Robert Munro, the Club Professional.

With just over 60 acres to play with, the problem was how best to cram a quart into a pint pot. Part of the solution was 'crossover' holes; the 8th crossing the 14th and the 11th; and the 16th crossing the 1st. It was also necessary to incorporate the ladies' course into the 18 holes. Mr. Devonshire's design shaped the fundamentals of today's layout. In future years some holes would be lengthened and more bunkers would be added but Mr Devonshire would still recognise the course.

June
1900
The extended
18-hole course
is opened

An 18-hole course

The new 18-hole course was opened for play in June 1900.

The lady members of the Club were given the right to play over the new course with forward tees, under certain restrictions as to their hours of play. The prohibition on Sunday golf, instigated by William Willett continued. By then the membership had grown to 117 men and 60 ladies. Subscriptions were still six guineas for men and three guineas for ladies, with entrance fees of five guineas and three guineas respectively.

At the Annual Dinner of June 1900 Mr Devonshire was installed as Captain for the coming year. After dinner, a cabaret was staged by members. This included a pianoforte selection, a flute solo and a violin solo. The new Captain sang *'The Lost Ball'* reported to be an amusing parody of his own based on *The Lost Chord*. It seems that a Chislehurst tradition of finding 'talent' amongst its members can be traced back at least this far.

Kent v Hampshire

The new course must have been in good condition very quickly. Only four months after it was opened, a ladies' county match was played on it. Kent ladies played Hampshire ladies.
Kent won by five points to three.

The Pit

The new 18-hole course would continue to evolve as changes were implemented over the years. The first alterations of any substance were carried out in 1908. The holes affected were the 9th and 14th and the alterations were once more designed by Mr. Easton Devonshire.

Originally the green for the 9th hole was somewhere around the level of the large tree on the right-hand side of the fairway, about 60 yards short of the present green. The plan was to lengthen the hole by moving the green to its present site but that position was occupied by an enclosure housing the six grass lawn tennis courts, one gravel court, a tennis pavilion and a path onto Camden Park Road. The courts were let on a short term basis to Chislehurst Lawn Tennis Ground Syndicate Ltd., who were given notice to vacate the site and the work of moving the green and tidying up the ground was carried out. Four new tennis courts were constructed for the syndicate further back towards the entrance. Two of these covered the position where the practice green is now sited.

The original green for the 14th green was further back down the fairway.

1908
The 9th and 14th holes are lengthened

1914
5 holes lengthened and 50 new bunkers added

The 1st fairway, 1910

James Braid (1870-1950)

James Braid was one of 'The Great Triumvirate' of Braid, Harry Vardon and J. H. Taylor. He was British Open Champion in 1901, 1905, 1906, 1908, and 1910 and pioneered the explosion shot from sandy bunkers. In 1912 he scaled back his tournament golf, became the Professional at Walton Heath Golf Club and built his reputation as a golf course architect, designing over 200 courses.

Longer holes, more bunkers and fewer sheep

In June 1914 very substantial alterations were completed, lengthening the 1st, 2nd, 11th, 12th, and 18th holes and adding some 50 new bunkers. Designed by the legendary James Braid, the work was supervised by F. G. Hawtree, who was at that time greenkeeper at Sundridge Park Golf Club but would later become famous as a golf course architect, working with A. J. Taylor. The company Hawtree founded in 1912 came back to work on the course in 2000.

As the new bunkers arrived the resident flock of 150 sheep left. The committee felt that the presence of sheep would *'not be conducive to good bunker management.'*

To commemorate the alterations an exhibition match took place on the 23 June 1914 between James Braid, Ernest Jones (the Chislehurst Professional), Tom Ball (Raynes Park) and Jacob Ross (Park Langley).

They played a medal round in the morning and foursomes in the afternoon. In the medal round, Braid took 73 against 68 by Jones, 65 by Ball and 66 by Ross. In mitigation of Braid's poor score it was ungenerously suggested that he wanted spectators to 'appreciate' the effectiveness of his positioning of the new bunkers.

Chislehurst golf today

The unintentional creation of a practice green

By 1927 the course yardage was recorded as 5,108 and further changes have done little to change it significantly. Today it measures a rather similar 5,106 yards.

In 1929 it was decided to lengthen the 9th hole again by moving the green onto the site of two of the four remaining tennis courts, where the practice green is now sited. This left the Chislehurst Lawn Tennis Club with only two courts and they made the decision to give these up soon afterwards. The necessary work was carried out in 1930 but in 1932 the committee decided that the old 9th green (i.e. the present green) should continue be used for competitions and that no application should be made for the Standard Scratch Score (SSS) in respect of the now lengthened 9th hole.

This strange decision created something of a problem. The old/original green had to be kept in good condition for competitions but, in order to reach the new green, it had to be to be played over the rest of the time. It didn't take long for the members to ignore the new green, reverting to the old green for all play and competition, leaving the redundant new green to be adopted as a practice green.

Aerial view 1929
© Historic Environment Scotland

The course still benefits from the work of those early designers. Tom Dunn, Easton Devonshire and James Braid individually and collectively provided strong foundations to build upon.

The 18th hole was unfortunately altered forever when the glorious cedar tree beside the green had to be removed in 1996. Other decisions over the years have been more deliberate and recent investments and works have raised the quality of the course in all respects. Major efforts have been made to improve irrigation and drainage starting with a £77,000 project in 1996 to establish a new sprinkler system. A new back tee was created on the 16th hole. The quality of the bunkers was addressed in 2000. Hawtrees, golf architects since 1912, with some 500 courses to their name, were appointed to renew, renovate and replace as required all the bunkers. The cost was £150,000. It was originally planned as a three year programme, but appalling weather delayed the works. Eventually the whole programme was completed in the winter months of 2001/02.

Professional green-staff and more investment

There was a very significant change in policy in 2003. Until then Chislehurst had not embraced the possibility of using professionally qualified green-staff, preferring to call in expert agronomists, as and when required. The quality of the course was not keeping up with modern trends and improvements in technology. That changed when Peter Gee was appointed as head greenkeeper in January 2003. He was followed by John Donelly in 2005 and by John Hunnisett in 2006. These gentlemen encouraged investment in better machinery, shaped fairways, graded the rough and created fairways and putting surfaces that are the envy of everyone around.

A continuous programme of investment in course machinery has been an essential part of the budgets from that time onwards. In 2005 alone the Club invested in 14 new machines on lease finance at an effective cost of £225,000. The results have been worthwhile. In winter months in recent years the course has been open more than other local courses and seems better able to withstand the various blights that constantly threaten golf courses such as fusarium.

Winter 2003/04 then saw the redesign of the 13th hole, removing the sand quarry. Much of the work was done by the in-house green-keeping team. The 7th hole was redesigned and reopened in the spring of 2013 with this work largely done by contractors. It was expensive but an undoubted success.

The irrigation system was extended to the 4th and 18th fairways, boreholes drilled at the 11th and beside the 18th and a new irrigation tank was installed in 2016 beside the 18th green, making the Club more self sufficient.

A further rolling bunker renovation programme was started in 2015, and is as yet unfinished. The cost per bunker is now nearly double that of the early 2000s. Although that original programme had resulted in better shaped bunkers, many had poor drainage and some did not have any membrane to stop stones surfacing. This latest expenditure should eliminate that problem, whilst the opportunity to remove some redundant bunkers has been taken and a few better-positioned traps have been laid.

Course records

At 5,106 yards for the men, the course may be short but a par and SSS of 66 gives nothing away. The challenge Chislehurst represents is evident when you consider that the amateur course record of 62 for a medal round, set in 1938 by O.J. Llewellyn, equalled by D.I. Nalder in 1964 remained for more than fifty years before being broken by J.D. Murray who carded a 61 in 1993. This record was equalled by Graham Kerr (2009) before being beaten in 2012 when Freddie Price shot 60 in the Kent Junior Championship hosted by the Club. That score was equalled by Liam Burns in 2016 and then beaten by him on 14 October 2018, when he scored a remarkable 58 in testing conditions. The professional course record stands at 59 by Anthony Tarchetti scored during a Pro-Am at CGC in 2008.

At 4,747 yards (SSS 69) the ladies' course is equally challenging. The course record of 67 was set by Jeanne Gibson in 1985. This was improved by one shot in 2009 by Lucy Matthews.

The professional course record of 62 was set by Ernest Jones in 1919 but alterations to the course meant that Alf Padgham's 64 in 1941 was recognised as a new record. It was lowered several times before Anthony Tarchetti became the first player to record a magical 59 at our Pro-Am in 2008, getting birdies on each of the last 5 holes.

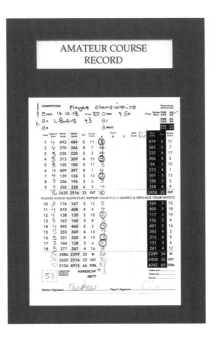

AMATEUR COURSE RECORD

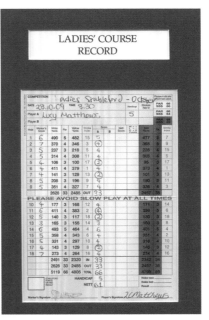

LADIES' COURSE RECORD

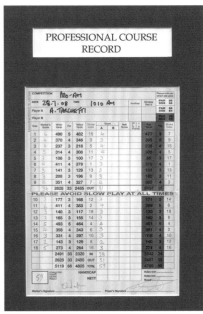

PROFESSIONAL COURSE RECORD

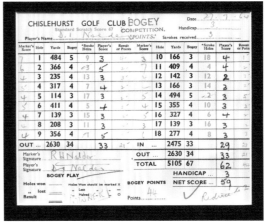

Aerial view 2018
© Google Earth

Camden Place Ltd. becomes Chislehurst Golf Club Ltd.

The name of the company changed to Chislehurst Golf Club Ltd. in 1998, one hundred years after Camden Place Ltd. had been incorporated on 5 August 1898. Michael Hollingsworth remembers that just as he took over the Chairmanship the company name was changed and we received a Certificate from the Companies Registry commemorating the centenary of the registration of the original Company. This was the equivalent of a royal telegram.

Camden Place Lodge

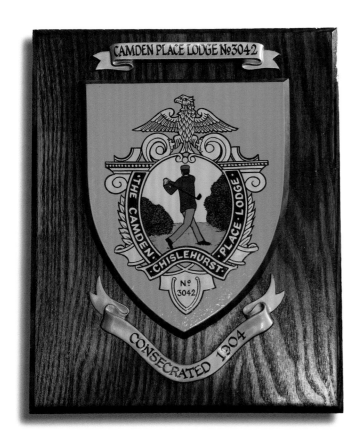

Camden Place is not only the home of Chislehurst Golf Club. For 115 years it has also been the home of Camden Place Lodge which was consecrated on Monday 27 June 1904 by the then Provincial Grand Master Earl Amhurst in the dining room at Camden Place where the Lodge still meets. Today it is one of 180 Lodges in West Kent but it is unique in that for over 100 years it has met in the same building, save for two meetings in 1944 after the building had been damaged by enemy action.

The Lodge was formed for the benefit of members of the Club (of the first 22 members, most were golfers, including the then captain, his immediate predecessor and successor) and the original by-laws provided that 50% of the members should come from the Club. That rule has been relaxed but we still seek to bolster our ranks from Club members, not least to strengthen our team in the annual golf match against the Club each July.

Freemasonry is a fraternal, secular, charitable society, open to all men who have a belief in a Supreme Being. However, the discussion of religion and politics, which so often cause division, are strictly prohibited in our meetings. You may have seen the room prepared for our meetings and must have noticed the black and white chequered carpet.

This is to remind us of the joys and sorrows, the light and the dark, of our chequered existence on earth.

It meets four times a year in October, December, February and March, and also has some social events. A typical meeting consists of a business element such as minutes, accounts, proposals for charity, and reports on absent members, together with a ceremony of ritual. This takes the form of a play during which a candidate becomes a Freemason and starts on the great journey of self-discovery that lies at the heart of masonry.

Today the 40 plus members are but a small part of the Province of West Kent. There are around 4,500 members in our small part of Kent which roughly is the area of the Kentish Men, to the west of the Medway. However, we are proud that Camden Place is regarded as one of the most eminent Lodges in the Province, as indeed our much loved Club is so highly regarded in our local area.

The Lodge congratulates the Club on the completion of 125 years bringing joy and happiness to the membership. In just ten years we too will complete our first 125 years and we hope will long continue in 'the grand design of being happy and communicating happiness'.

R.W. Bro Jonathan Stewart Winpenny

Provincial Grand Master of the Province of West Kent, 2005–2015.

Contents

THE DOINGS
OF THE
CHISLEHURST GOLF CLUB

3

125 years of 'The Doings of the Chislehurst Golf Club'

In the archives of the Club Bill Mitchell found a leather bound volume 'The Doings of the Chislehurst Golf Club'. It had only a few entries from the 30s and 40s but the 'doings' seem to be a great description for the general life of the Club.

For 125 years Chislehurst has provided generations of members with plenty 'to do', a focal point for their golf, leisure and social activity. Its continuing success can be attributed to the collective energies and efforts of members both on and off the course. This section focuses on some of the highlights, events and people who have shaped the Club.

The first 20 years: 1894–1913

This was one of the most important periods for golf in the UK. The 1890s was the decade when the English caught the bug and Chislehurst was just one of many new clubs fuelling golf fever. The first 10 years were busy ones as the Club became established. In 1894 Chislehurst Golf Club was opened with William Willett Junior as the proprietor. Within five years Camden Place Ltd. was set up and the property and proprietorship of the golf club purchased from the Willetts.

Once the Club was in control of its own destiny after 1899 there followed years of consolidation and growth, most notably with the course extended from 9 to 18 holes necessitating the early loss of the ladies course.

Time-poor golfers then and now

Throughout this period membership grew steadily, despite the proprietor William Willett banning Sunday play, a restriction initially maintained even when Camden Place Ltd. took over. Many of those early members would have had limited experience of the game and it is hard to imagine just when many of the men got to play or practise. At this time the typical work week finished at lunch time on Saturday and with no Sunday play it must have been hard for the working members to find much time on the course. Nonetheless the Club quickly established itself on the Kent golf scene. There is no record of when this play restriction was lifted but no serious golf matches were scheduled on the Sunday until 1930.

A social hub

Those early years must have been quite special at Camden Place and golf was not the only attraction at that time. A round in the morning could be followed by a game of croquet, a few sets of tennis and then afternoon tea in the glass conservatory, and if the weather was bad there were squash, billiards or bridge available.

On weekday afternoons Miss Pearce, Miss Rampton and Mr Douglas Logan, were among those competing for rooms in which to give dancing lessons. Small dances were frequent and room hire varied from ten to twenty guineas. The annual Chislehurst Golf Club Ball took place in January and during the winter concerts of chamber music were regular Saturday night events.

Not surprisingly CGC quickly established itself as both a family club and a social hub. Whole families joined as members, even if they did not all play golf.

July
1895
J.H. Taylor and Dan Bryson jointly set a course record of 35

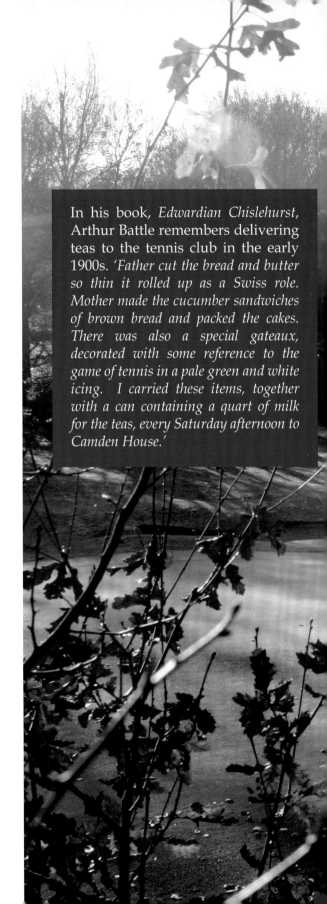

In his book, *Edwardian Chislehurst*, Arthur Battle remembers delivering teas to the tennis club in the early 1900s. '*Father cut the bread and butter so thin it rolled up as a Swiss role. Mother made the cucumber sandwiches of brown bread and packed the cakes. There was also a special gateaux, decorated with some reference to the game of tennis in a pale green and white icing. I carried these items, together with a can containing a quart of milk for the teas, every Saturday afternoon to Camden House.*'

1894
Dan Bryson
is Club Professional

1899
Robert Munro
is Club Professional

Early Professionals

Bryson (1894–1899) and Munro (1899–1902)

When the Club opened under William Willett's proprietorship the Professional appointed was Dan Bryson, whose tenure ended in 1899 when the Club changed hands and Camden Place Ltd. was set up. The new management committee appointed Robert Munro, who only remained until 1902.

Dan Bryson and Mr H.S. James on the 2nd green

Jack Youds (1902–1910)

In 1902, Jack Youds applied to join Chislehurst as a professional and caddy master for a fee of eighteen shillings per week. The fact he was already the third Professional appointed perhaps explains why the records indicate his welcome was on the cool side:

'We should like to know your age…. Your fees for teaching would be 2/6 per hour….

We would expect you to keep a reasonable stock of good balls, both new and remade.'

Youds had done well in the 1897 Open Championship and at Chislehurst he soon established a new professional course record of 62, two better than the amateur record shared by O.C. Bevan (1900) and C. E. Dick (1903). He remained the Club's Professional for over seven years and when he moved on he had clearly won over the membership. His hard work on the course included the creation of the new greens for the 9th and 14th holes which allowed the fairways to be lengthened. He received a glowing testimonial:

The Committee of the Chislehurst Golf Club wish to express to J. Youds their regret at his retirement from the Club. They have always found him the most valuable servant to the club, most straightforward and obliging in every way and an excellent teacher, a first rate club maker, hardworking on the course, in fact fulfilling every requirement a golf professional should possess.

85

Ladies golf takes off

The ladies were enthusiastic members and a cornerstone of golf at Chislehurst from day one. Initially they had their own, albeit very small, 9–hole course and a ladies' club room on the first floor.

In these early decades CGC ladies' golf was far from a Cinderella activity. The Club had several very good lady golfers, membership was strong and the ladies seem to have been more active than the men. They participated and hosted local and county matches. They supported Kent Golf from the beginning and in the first full season in 1900 Kent ladies came second to Surrey in the County Championship.

To a large extent it was the ladies of the club who put Chislehurst on the golfing map in Kent.

1910 and 1912
Mrs Jackson is Kent Amateur Champion

Lady Captains at Chislehurst

There are no official records of the Lady Captains of Chislehurst until 1935 but from then they are recorded on the honour boards in the hall. However, we know the ladies were a flourishing and very active group from 1894 and we have earlier mentions of both Secretary and Captain (for example Mrs Marsham-Townshend is known to have been Lady Captain in 1927), so it is certain they had their own structure within the wider club.

The ladies' handicap

Ladies did however have an extra handicap. As can be seen image of Mrs L. Jackson. Ladies' attire wasn't altogether suited for the game in those early days; a skirt that was several inches off the ground and a simple blouse. A full swing of the club was hindered by the blouse sleeves that were too fitted and the skirt often caught the club as it swept by.

Bromley Telegraph
October 8, 1910

GOLF.

On the Chislehurst Club's course, on Saturday, the annual tournament for the ladies' championship of Kent ended in favour of Mrs. Lionel Jackson, who, in the final of 18 holes, defeated Miss D. Evans by 3 and 2. Miss Evans, after losing the first hole, might have won the second and third holes, but she missed putts and could only halve. She became 2 down at the fourth through a sliced drive, and 3 down at the fifth, where she was again weak on the green. Miss Evans won the seventh in 2, but lost the next two holes, and turned 4 down. Mrs. Jackson was out in 41 strokes, as against her opponent's 44. Mrs. Jackson was bunkered at the tenth, and she lost her ball from a sliced shot at the eleventh. Her lead was thus reduced to 2, but she held her own from that point, and proved successful as stated.

Mrs Lionel Jackson, the winner of the Kent County Ladies' Golf Championship, playing at Chislehurst October 8th 1910

Photo: London News Agency

Dispersing a financial cloud

Despite the steady growth of members and the social activities at Camden Place, a financial cloud hung over the Club. Interest payments on the debenture loans were not always made and the repayment of the principal sums were due for repayment in a rapidly approaching 1911. By July 1908 it was clear that repayment of the capital was not a possibility. Mr Travers Hawes, by now Chairman of Camden Place Ltd., summoned a meeting of debenture holders and suggested a 20 year postponement of the repayment date. Once more his arguments prevailed.

By November only 25 needed reminding to submit their debentures for endorsement. William Willett was one of those slow to respond, despite the fact that his father's Second Mortgage Debenture of £3,000 had never received any interest payments. His complaints in 1911 fell on unsympathetic ears. The Secretary, Evan Edwards, simply pointed out that after lengthy discussions the motion to extend the First Debentures had been carried by a significant majority. In the end the Second Debenture was redeemed from Willett Snr. for £2,000. The cash to do this was raised by a new mortgage which took priority over the First Debentures, although these details were not publicised at the time.

The sheep come and go

Sheep were a feature of Camden Place from the beginning. They were considered important in managing the rough, where horse-drawn machines couldn't cope and the sheep were preferred to scythes. They were also a source of income. By 1910 the farmer, W.F. Hobbs of Romney Marsh, was paying £1 a week rent.

In that year and just 10 days before the Ladies Spring Meeting, Mr Hobbs removed his 150 sheep from the course, saving himself the rent of £52 for the year. There was an outcry and the farmer was implored to bring the sheep back, enticed by the waiving of the rent. He agreed and subsequently it seems the golf went well.

*Available from
Skylane Publishing*

Ernest Jones
Professional (1910–1924)

Ernest Jones before the War

In 1906 Jack Youds got an 18-year-old assistant who quickly broke his course record of 62 by a shot. That assistant, Ernest Jones, would go on to become an internationally renowned teacher of golf to both amateurs and professionals. In 1910 he took over as the Club Professional, a post he held until 1924.

In 1914 Jones volunteered for service, serving in the Sportsman's Battalion of the Royal Fusiliers. In March 1916 he lost his right leg just below the knee at the Battle of Vimy Ridge. Understandably he was afraid this would be the end to his career as a professional golfer. Overcoming his injury with no impairment to his golfing ability convinced Jones that it was the correct movement of the club head, rather than of body parts, that was the key to golf.

On his return to playing at Chislehurst he broke the course record twice within a two-week period in July 1919, scoring a 63 then a 62 (the course having been lengthened and upgraded by the Braid bunkers since Jack Youds' day.) Jones was lured away by Marion Hollins to the Women's National Golf and Tennis Club, Long Island, New York and had a teaching facility on the 7th floor of A. G. Spaulding & Bros on 5th Avenue. He died in 1965 and was inducted in the World Golf Teachers' Hall of Fame in 1977.

Ernest Jones on the way to recovery

1910
Ernest Jones
appointed
Club Professional

The war years: 1914–1918

By the beginning of 1914 things were going well for Chislehurst. The now 18-hole course was in good condition and recent improvements had included 50 new bunkers, designed by James Braid. The sheep had been given notice to quit in order to ensure good bunker management. Ernest Jones, an exceptional professional, was in post and Camden Place provided a social focus for the area. The debenture repayment problem had been put on hold until 1931. Everything seemed settled at last.

War time changes

War heralded a much more difficult time for the Club and the country. Understandably, golf matters were largely put on hold, evidenced by the fact that A.N. Lubbock was elected Captain in 1914 and he held the fort until a new Captain, R.A. Brown, was elected in 1918. Only a few records exist from this time but it is clear that to keep the Club functioning changes were inevitable.

The war effort for CGC included allowing the sheep to return and turning over some 1.5 acres of land near Willow Grove for allotments. Members, including Professional Ernest Jones, signed up.

The financial impact is evident in the accounts. Subscription income fell from £1,658 to £917. The accounts presented in the AGM on 23 July 1914 showed total revenues of £2,987; by October 1918 revenue had fallen to £1,884 (less than the £2,128 recorded in 1911).

The croquet club became a casualty of war.

Chislehurst Lads Leaving for The Front, July 10th 1915

Less energy

The following archive extract gives us some sense of the impact on day-to-day club life. An inspector was sent to check up on a suspiciously low reading from the electricity meter and the Secretary wrote to explain:

10.8.1915

'This it is an entirely abnormal year owing to the war. For instance we have only two persons lodging in the house instead of five last year, we have a smaller staff, fewer members using the club, no golf meetings and no annual dinner. We're also using the small dining room in place of the large one and there is no billiard tournament.'

1914
Fifty new bunkers designed by James Braid

90

A period of change: 1919-1929

Society had changed by 1918. Women had contributed to the war effort. Those over 30 were given the vote and by 1928 this was extended to all women over 21. It was the roaring twenties. People wanted to enjoy the post-war peace. At Chislehurst gradually things started to improve. Ernest Jones was once more in the Pro's shop and members returned to the Club.

Income and costs increase

Money had to be spent on the course and clubhouse, including repairs to the roof which cost £800. Income levels bounced back to £3,547 in 1920 but the expenditure on the house and course continued and by 1921 there was a reported loss of £1,213.

On 29 September 1922 the Company purchased the four acre site (today the area that encompasses the 3rd fairway and green and the 4th tee and the allotments beside them). Also a lease was signed on the land that is now the 4th green, which was eventually purchased on 28 June 1954.

New member marketing campaign

To address the post-war income shortfall, 1923 saw a recruitment drive which attracted 92 new members (with only 17 resignations that year). Golf was still a popular activity.

The death of Travers Hawes

On Tuesday 20 May 1924, Alexander Travers Hawes died at the age of 73. He was buried at St Nicholas Church, surrounded by the common he had loved and defended so successfully.

Chislehurst Golf Club owes an enormous amount to this man. He had been at the centre of all local affairs in Chislehurst for 40 years and due to his imagination and skills, the golf club came into existence. He was the brains behind the financial model that helped forge the Club's independence and has ensured its continuation. He was the longest serving Chairman, leading the Club from 1906–1924.

The Club ensured he would be remembered by naming the handicap medal round at the autumn meeting the Travers Hawes Prize. This was renamed the Travers Hawes Bowl in 1934 when his widow returned to the Club the bowl they had presented to Travers Hawes at the 1899 luncheon to celebrate the purchase of the Club.

Social success adds to financial loss

The Annual Cricket Week Ball was a firm fixture in the social calendar for West Kent cricketers and Chislehurst golfers. The popularity was undiminished by 1920 when 195 tickets were sold. The charge was 30 shillings for the men and 25 shillings for the ladies. This was at a time when the average weekly wage was about £5.

The Royal Artillery band provided the music and the evening was deemed a great success but it still made a loss of £13. 18s.

1922
Willow Grove land purchased

1924
Travers Hawes dies

92

Handicaps

Handicaps are always a problem with a short course. As early as 1908 *Nisbett's Golf Year Book* makes that point in respect of Chislehurst:

'The 18 holes have been carefully laid out, but the course is unfortunately too short for modern driving.'

For many years each golf club fixed its own handicap and it was only between 1921 and 28, many years after the Ladies Golf Union had tackled the problem, that the Royal &Ancient made an attempt to encourage some degree of overall comparability. To act as a guide the scratch score at each of six championship courses was fixed at 79. These courses were St Andrew's, Prestwick, Muirfield, Hoylake, Sandwich and Deal. On 2 May 1925 Chislehurst informed the R&A that the scratch score was to be 70. In time the R&A passed the problem to the English Golf Union and Kent Golf Union, starting more years of negotiation between the relevant organisations until the scratch score was finally reduced to 67 in 1938.

Golfing success

A TRIUMPH FOR YOUTH.
Mr. Rex Hartley and Mr. W. L. Hartley, who, representing Chislehurst, won the London Amateur Foursomes at Addington last week. Their opponents in the final, which they won by 5 and 4, were the Woking representatives, Mr. E. B. H. Blackwell, who is 62 years of age, and Mr. Bernard Darwin, who was playing for England in international matches 26 years ago. This was Chislehurst's third win in six years.

1923
Hartley Brothers win their first London Amateur

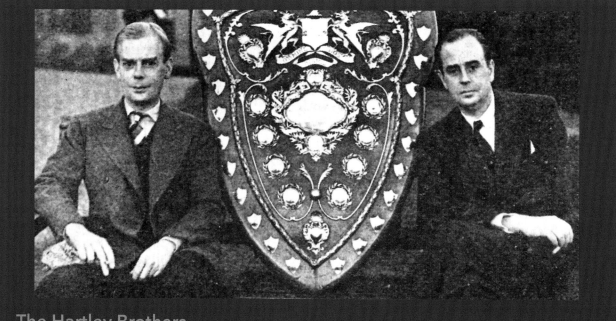

The Hartley Brothers

In 1923 Club members Lister and Rex Hartley won the prestigious London Amateur Foursomes for the first of what would be three wins in six years. Eventually they would have four victories in 16 years, the last being in 1938.

Aged just 18 and 19, the brothers had benefited from Ernest Jones's tuition and individually their success in championship golf between 1923 and 1938 was significant. Rex played in the 1930 Walker Cup at Royal St. Georges and both brothers played in the 1932 Walker Cup at Brookline, near Boston U.S.A. They still number amongst Chislehurst's most successful men players. In 1924 when they won at The Addington, *The Times* had this to say about them.

'They play a foursome in a way that is a pleasure to witness, with obvious reliance upon one another, and with the closest collaboration and sympathy, and at the same time wasting no time in fruitless searches for putting formulae or exploration of avenues to the hole….   Mr R.W. had the most of the crucial putts to hole and holed them time after time. His long game is not quite so good as that of his elder brother, who has a beautifully true, round, smooth swing, he more than did his bit, and indeed both deserve all the praises one can give them.'

The Perman Shield

From the earliest days, golf matches between local clubs were popular. Chislehurst appears to have been an active participant. Local inter-club matches were given a focus when in 1925 J.E. Perman of Sundridge Park Golf Club inaugurated the Perman Shield competition, to be played amongst clubs in the vicinity of Bromley, Kent. The original contestants were Sundridge Park, Langley Park, Chislehurst, Bromley & Bickley, Royal Blackheath, West Kent, Foxgrove and Sidcup.

Perman's idea was a good one that has stood the test of time and indeed been extended. These days Royal Blackheath administer a complete set of match-play team events for clubs in the northwest corner of Kent. Selected from a stated handicap range, teams of eight compete in match play on level terms. Enthusiasm and competition for these local trophies remain strong, with members spectating and caddying for their team and enjoying the victory celebrations when they come along. Chislehurst were losing finalists in the first three years of the competition but in 1929 and 1930 Chislehurst won and then retained the Perman Shield.

The 1966 victorious Perman Shield Team

1924
Alf Bunce appointed
Club Professional

1929 and 1930
CGC
wins Perman Shield

1931
A.G. Wallis appointed
Club Professional

Ladies golf

Whilst the Hartley brothers were making their mark on the men's golf scene, Chislehurst ladies remained prominent at club, county and country levels.

At this time there was no Ladies' Open at Chislehurst but in March 1922 the Club did play host to the first London Ladies' Foursomes. From an entry of 38, West Hill came out as winners in an exciting finish. Chislehurst failed to qualify for the knockout section, which required a score of 92. The following year Chislehurst ladies played better, with Mrs Kay Morrice and Mrs L. Jackson surviving for two rounds, before losing to Sunningdale by 5 and 4.

Chislehurst was in regular use for ladies' county matches during these years and the lady members took on key county roles. Mrs Jackson was succeeded as Captain of Kent in 1924 by Mrs Morrice. Both ladies played for their countries, Mrs Jackson for Ireland and Mrs Morrice for England. Miss Doxford was another Chislehurst lady who captained

the county, winning the Kent Championship in 1927 and again in 1932. She later became President of Kent and started a junior competition, the Doxford Trophy, which remains on the KCLGA annual diary.

In 1929 Chislehurst won the Pearson Trophy for the first and so far the only time. They were at the pinnacle of Kent ladies' amateur golf, demonstrated by winning the Ladies' Golf Union Shield on eight separate occasions, with the Jackson family, Mrs Doxford and Mrs Morrice featuring strongly. The five winning years between the wars were 1921, 1933, 1936, 1937 and 1938.

LADY CAPTA

1935	Mrs. T.L.H.JACKS
1936	Miss J.MANSEL
1937	Miss R.BROWN
1938	Miss B.M.JACKS
1939/45	Mrs. R.T.HAWES
1946	Mrs. L.SIMPSON
1947	Mrs. J.K.WELLS
1948	Mrs. D.R.LANG.
1949	Mrs. H.C.PYNE.
1950	Mrs. M.R.MARS
1951	Mrs. A.E.O'DON
1952	Mrs. E.W.GANDE
1953	Mrs. A.J.SOMER
1954	Mrs. E.B.WRIGH
1955	Mrs. J.R.G.BART
1956	The Hon. Mrs. R.C.HU
1957	Mrs. A.W.INGLIS
1958	Mrs. G.R.EDEY.
1959	Mrs. C.W.ASTEL
1960	Mrs. K.H.NALDE

FREDA JACKSON CUP

1935	MRS. D.R. LANG.
1936	MRS. E.M. GRACEY.
1937	MISS P.M. MITCHELL.
1938	MRS. F.C. HALSE.
1947	MRS. D.R. LANG.
1948	MRS. D.R. LANG.
1949	MRS. K.H. NALDER.
1950	MRS. M.R. MARSHAL.
1951	MRS. A.H. OGDEN.
1952	MRS. E.M. FRENCH.
1953	MISS D.E. BOLTON.
1954	MRS. K.H. NALDER.
1955	MRS. P.K. CLAPHAM.
1956	MISS D.E. BOLTON.
1957	MRS. E.M. CASWELL.
1958	MRS. C.W. ASTELL.
1959	MRS. A.C. GLENDINNING.
1960	MISS R. BROWN.
1961	MRS. M.G. BATEMAN.
1962	MRS. C.T. STACEY.

*The original
Pearson Trophy*

The Pearson Trophy

Miss Issette Pearson, who had co-founded the Ladies Golf Union and was runner-up in the first two British Ladies' Amateur Championships, presented the cup in 1910 for clubs in Hertfordshire, Kent, Middlesex and Surrey for those with handicaps 1–24. In 1922 this was changed and competed for by intermediate golfers (handicaps 13 to 30), and then in 2007 the handicap range was again extended to 13–32. A round-robin of internal matches produces a winner from each county who goes on to finals day.

Another change for the debenture holders

Travers Hawes was succeeded as Chairman of Camden Place Ltd. by Dr James White. In 1927 he pre-empted the need for redemption of debentures in July 1931 by ensuring they were declared perpetual. To soften this blow the interest paid to the debenture holders was to be increased to $3\frac{1}{2}\%$ for a few years. This action dealt with the risk posed by an underlying problem. Over the years more and more of the original debentures were being passed on through inheritance, often to people not necessarily interested in maintaining golf at Chislehurst. In 1932 it was estimated that only about half of the 184 full playing members held shares.

1929
Ladies win
the Pearson Trophy

The 30s: 1929-1938

The financial crash of 1929 heralded the Great Depression and had ramifications for all. It meant a lot of belt-tightening. By the mid-1930s the Company was again financially insecure.

Chislehurst was not alone in feeling the pinch at this time. Other clubs in the area suffered a drop in full playing membership and were forced to reduce their subscriptions. Clubs were living a hand-to-mouth existence. At Chislehurst this meant not much could be done around the clubhouse.

In 1936 the Secretary regretted that the overdraft was nearing £500 and in July 1937 he was authorised to negotiate the sale of £300 of debentures and twelve shares at £42.10s, an all-time low. When the drive to Camden Place had to be resurfaced in 1937, the cost of £212. 6s was covered by voluntary contributions from just a few members.

Catering in the clubhouse showed a loss and an increase in subscription rates was out of the question. Suspending the entrance fees helped to attract some new members, something that many decades later again became a prevalent tactic used by clubs chasing membership numbers.

Golf remained popular

Club membership was still good value for money, particularly for the ladies who paid just five guineas a year. Medals were played on the first and third Thursday of each month and the men were happy to welcome ladies to their bogey competition on the second Saturday. To play the ladies added six to the LGU handicaps and used the men's white tees.

Neighbouring clubs played together and were careful not to clash. Royal Blackheath had its ladies' medal on a Tuesday, Bromley & Bickley on a Wednesday, and Langley Park on a Friday. There was certainly plenty of golf available and by 1929 Chislehurst had a complement of 125 full-playing lady members, who were making better use of the course than the men.

> In 1932, although the scoring was excellent, the men's autumn meeting still only had 39 entrants on the Saturday and 34 on the Sunday.

Ladies at the 19th

In 1932 one structural alteration was made to the house. The bar, which was situated in what is now the front office, acquired a second door, half way towards the billiard room. This door divided into halves; the upper half could be opened independently for the convenience of any lady member who wanted to order a drink for herself and not wait for gentlemen to bring one out to her. The resulting increase in turnover is not recorded.

Bridge membership

In January 1936 bridge membership was introduced at two guineas a year and was very popular. Monday-only subscription of one guinea rapidly swelled the Bridge Club numbers to 50. Card money of one shilling was payable each time one played.

Changing attitudes towards the ladies

In January 1936, apparently as part of a cost-saving exercise, the ladies were informed that in future the inter-club matches should be limited to two teams of seven players a side, 14 players in all, inclusive of the lady members of Chislehurst. It was also decided that the Club would only provide ten free teas a year for their opposing teams.

More changes were to follow and in 1937 the ladies were prohibited from playing on Sunday mornings, unless accompanied by a man. The status of ladies on the course at weekends was to be further constrained in 1949.

1938 a new Professional needed

F.S. Marsh did not have a good start to his year as captain. On his first day in the post the Professional, A.G. Wallis, died suddenly, leaving his widow in very difficult circumstances. The membership of the Club had a collection and provided enough cash to support her for a year with a balance that could be deposited with the public trustee.

Within the month on Saturday 18 June Sydney Mason, who had previously been Ernest Jones' assistant, took up the post of Club Professional. He was delighted to be back working with his old friend George Brewster, who was the green-keeper. Between them they had the Chislehurst Artisans Golf Club up and running in good time for Christmas.

Sydney Mason

Mason was Chislehurst born and bred. His family owned the fishmongers on the High Street, Ince and Masons. His father did all the sign-writing at CGC from 1894 till his death in 1954.

Sydney had caught Ernest Jones' eye in 1914 and taken on to work in the shop in 1916. In 1928 he became a full Professional at Honor Oak, then Eltham Warren but his heart was at Chislehurst.

An excellent teacher, having learned from Ernest Jones, he was fundamental in building a strong junior membership and would inspire many golfers until his retirement in 1974. He taught the juniors in his Friday morning group classes. Most would forever remember his mantra that 'the clubhead is like a weight on a piece of string; never swing too quickly or the string will crumple'.

Noteworthy results

On the 25 September 1938, O.J. Llewellyn set up a new amateur course record of 62 and Chislehurst won the Perman Shield for the first time since the double of 1929 and 1930. This 1938 side contained 2 Hartleys and 2 Jacksons but O.J. Llewellyn did not play.

Miss Bridget Jackson

Like her mother, Bridget Jackson played for Ireland in 1937, 1938, 1939 and 1950. In 1938 she was Lady Captain of Chislehurst. In 1939 she was runner-up in the Irish Ladies' Amateur Championship and a semi-finalist in 1959. She won the Kent Ladies' Championship in 1939, 1950, 1951, and 1952 and the South Eastern Ladies' Championship in 1954. Miss Jackson was Lady Captain of Kent in 1951 and 1952 and President of Kent from 1973 to 1977.

Although the 30s had been a challenging decade financially for everyone, full-playing membership remained fairly stable throughout, ending in 1939 with 178 men and 118 ladies.

1938
Sydney Mason appointed Club Professional

Another war: 1939-1945

By 1939 things were once again well under control at Camden Place. All the rooms were let, the debenture holders had received their dividends on time and the Company felt brave enough to increase subscription rates for new members to nine guineas for men and six for ladies. The clubhouse was repainted at a cost of £101.5s and golfers were once more having success.

As Bill Mitchell highlighted in his book for the centenary, 'the parallels with 1914 were all too close!' For a second time, war was going to impact on Camden Place just when the Club seemed to have everything going for it.

Facing the prospect of another war so soon after the last must have been daunting and so many members had first-hand experience of the horrors and disruption of war. This time the CGC Directors were determined not to let things slide.

There are more records of events during this time and whilst full-playing members were away on active duty, others were billeted at the Club or close by, providing an alternative source of income in exchange for Camden Park facilities. By 1942, 59 men (more than one in four of the members of the Club) were serving in His Majesty's Forces as were 12 of the ladies.

Temporary guests

Members of the Honourable Artillery Company (HAC) anti-aircraft battery billeted locally were given full use of the clubhouse and were able to play golf for one shilling a round. This concession was soon extended to all serving officers. Under the supervision of Mrs. Marsham–Townshend of Scadbury (Lady Captain 1927), members of the ATS based in Camden Park Road were also permitted to play, starting at the 12th.

In May 1940 Camden Place became the official headquarters of the 54th battalion, Kent Home Guard and very welcome guests they were. Besides the green fee income these visitors generated, they paid rent of £52 for the small dining room, which had been formally requisitioned, and were offered the squash court free, for use as a miniature shooting range.

Only four months later the gallant 54th had the distinction of bringing down a Dornier bomber on 18 August. The citation refers to the expenditure of 180 rounds of small arms ammunition. It is not now clear whether this implied praise for their enthusiasm or blame for their inaccuracy.

When not shooting down enemy aircraft these visitors were responsible for organising a number of social and sporting activities including several Home Guard golf days. Their activities ensured golf continued at the Club. For War Weapons Week in May 1941 they arranged an exhibition match between A. H. Padgham and Sam King. Padgham went round in 64 and King in 65. The good cause benefited to the tune of £58.

Snooker matches, dinners and occasional dances enlivened the blacked-out clubhouse and must have given some relief in the darker days of the war.

Keeping CGC functioning

A number of people played their part in keeping things running at Camden Place, efforts that were in keeping with the spirit of wartime Britain. The Herculean task of organising black-out curtains for the public rooms was taken on by Mrs Critchley and, when Sydney Mason was called up in 1941, his wife kept the shop open for the modest salary of one shilling a week. The West Kent Cricket Club's groundsman, George Strait, helped out on the greens and tees. After realising that subscription income had fallen from £2,413 to £1,462 the Secretary, George Ferguson, insisted that his salary be reduced by a fifth.

Charles Mitchell stayed on as Captain for the first two years of the war, to be followed by Charles Fletcher who came back to the office he had held in 1933. He continued as Captain until 1945. Mrs Roderick Travers Hawes looked after the ladies section as Lady Captain from 1939 to 1945.

Company Director Mr Nevill Christopherson could not attend meetings in person as he was prisoner 1585 in Stalag Vll but he appears to have kept in touch by post.

The war years brought tangible changes to the club as well. Railway sleepers embedded in concrete provided extra hazards on the 1st, 2nd, 4th, 6th, 14th and 16th fairways.

On several occasions in the autumn of 1940 Camden Place suffered minor damage, mainly broken windows, from enemy action, whilst in November 1940 the 8th and 11th holes were closed for play as a result of bomb damage. There may or may not have been an unexploded bomb to the left of the 1st fairway but to the end of his days Sydney Mason warned golfers against taking divots in that area.

CHISLEHURST GOLF CLUB.

DEAR SIR,

H.M. Forces.

I have been directed to inform you that the Committee has decided to offer to Officers of all Services the opportunity of becoming temporary Non-Playing Members of this Club at the reduced subscription of one Guinea per quarter (payable in advance) on application being made to the Secretary.

Admission under this decision may begin at any date.

As from 1st May, Honorary Non-Playing Membership which was conferred upon Officers at the outbreak of War, under conditions which no longer prevail, will terminate.

Yours faithfully,

The pit at the 7th resounded to the noise of the Home Guard pistol practice and sadly the railings and famous Strode Gates were given up to the war effort in early 1943.

The Home Guard Cup

In December 1944 the Home Guard left Camden Place marking the occasion with a parade in the driveway, followed by a party hosted jointly by C.E. Fletcher as Club Captain and J.H. Crewdson Howard, Chairman of Camden Place Ltd. Lieutenant Colonel Hodder Williams presented the Home Guard Cup to the Club, to be played for in an annual competition on a date as near to the 15 May as possible. It was stipulated that even if won by the same person on three successive years it was still to remain at Camden Place.

1944
the Home Guard Cup
presented to CGC

Recovery: 1945-1955

As in 1914–18, CGC had just about managed to survive the challenges war brought but it was in a sorry state. Those who had kept things going during the war were themselves ready to be relieved. The Chairman would turn 80 in September 1948 and the majority of the Board were nearing 70. The task they faced to get the house, course and finances back in order was immense.

Finances were shaky

By the end of the war membership numbers had fallen – there were 153 full-time men members, down from 178 in 1939. The ladies suffered much worse with only 57 full-playing members at the end of the war, down from 118 in 1939. The debenture holders had received no interest since the second year of the war, there was a permanent overdraft at Martin's Bank and Mr Faber had bailed Camden Place Ltd. out for a few months with an interest-free loan of £1,250. To help with the finances, subscriptions were raised at the AGM in 1946 to twelve guineas for men and eight for ladies.

War damage documents from the archive

Getting back to normal

The course could be cleared without too much expense but the house was a different matter. The roof had only been partially restored and the main dining room was not really fit for use. Repairs to the war damage were going to be expensive and the country was still struggling with rationing and a shortage of materials and resources. Seven years were to pass before the clubhouse was finally put to rights and many more than that before the finances of the Company were restored to equilibrium.

Another Travers Hawes takes the helm

At the AGM in May 1945, C. E. Fletcher proposed Roderick Travers Hawes as his successor. Roderick like his father had a keen interest in the wider affairs of Chislehurst but he was a more active sportsman than his father. His golf handicap had been 11 in 1931, he had rowed for Oxford and was a good squash player.

Roderick Travers Hawes recognised the importance of cricket on the Common as a focal point of local life. When the Band of Brothers, a wandering cricket side founded in 1858, returned to Chislehurst Common on the 1 September 1945 to play West Kent C.C., he organized a grand luncheon party at Camden Place, attended by the Lord Lieutenant of Kent and the President of the M.C.C.

Champagne and gin flowed

In 1946 when he had passed the captaincy of the Golf Club into the safe hands of R. E. Attenborough, Roderick Travers Hawes was able to join the committee of West Kent and immediately took charge of arrangements for the Cricket Week and its ball, still held at Camden Place.

The *Kentish Times* had much to say about the week being the sporting and social highlight of Chislehurst. The ball now became profitable as well as popular. In 1949 Messers Spicer and Pegler provided the first ever set of formal accounts for the event which reveal that 183 revellers disposed of:

96 bottles of Bollinger

36 bottles of Vouvray

24 bottles of La Dame Blanche

33 bottles of Gordon's gin.

No mention was made of red wine.

Three key staff

The efforts and contributions of the members have always been important to the Club but the full-time staff play a crucial role in generating, building and maintaining the Club atmosphere and values. Recovering from the war in the late 40s, 1950s and 60s the Club benefited from the work of three people, Captain Sinclair, Emmerson and Sydney Mason, who served the club over many years. This team provided structure and continuity and were central in shaping CGC and ensuring its recovery.

The Sydney Mason Rose Bowl

Captain E.W. Sinclair

The 'Commander,' was appointed Secretary in April 1947 and stayed in that post until his retirement on the grounds of ill health in September 1958, though he still came back to help out until 1962. His steady hand on Club operations was key to recovering from the war-time damage.

Sydney Mason

Club Professional before the war, Mason returned in 1946 to take up his role and he quickly established a Friday morning school for the juniors. Girls and boys came from quite a distance, each paying one shilling. Mason was another excellent teacher and did much to encourage juniors into the game of golf and these morning classes were hugely popular.

In 1950, when the first Kent Junior Championship to be held was played at Chislehurst, Anthea Marshall won the

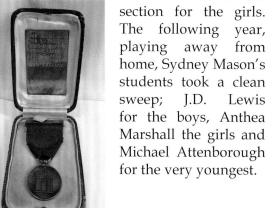

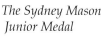

section for the girls. The following year, playing away from home, Sydney Mason's students took a clean sweep; J.D. Lewis for the boys, Anthea Marshall the girls and Michael Attenborough for the very youngest.

The Sydney Mason Junior Medal

Leslie T. Emmerson

Emmerson took over as steward from R.C. Nelms in 1947, although he had worked in the club in the 30s. It was said that a member's standing in the Club could be measured by the time it took for Emmerson to notice him at the bar.

In Bill Mitchell's book, Emmerson is remembered by John Attenborough.

'He was a character in every sense of the word. Short of stature, a man with a round, bouncy figure, mournful eyes and malleable features which registered domestic triumph and disaster with the comic genius of a Tony Hancock, Emmerson seemed to stem actually from the Upstairs Downstairs world. No one ever called him by his Christian name. He arrived at Camden Place immediately after the Second World War, having served with the Royal Navy. Whether his training began in the wardroom or in one of the great houses of England, he managed to display a positive Jeeves-like skill in handling the endless crises of the post-war years.'

Ernest Jones supported the juniors. Encouragement and support for junior golf is embedded at Chislehurst, substantially because of the work of the Professionals over the decades. That support was not just limited to their tenure at the club. Ernest Jones never lost his interest in the goings-on at Chislehurst. When he heard about Sydney Mason's Friday morning academy in 1949 he sent a cheque for £100 to purchase four silver cups, to be competed for in the autumn by older and younger boys and girls.

The Past Captains' Dinner

C. E. Fletcher, who had held the fort through most of the war years, now set the wheels in motion for the annual Past Captains' Dinner. In 1947 he gave a dinner to which all past captains of Chislehurst were invited, along with some from elsewhere. The idea stuck and after some years developed into the present fixed feast in November, where the current Captain is entertained by his predecessors and formally thanked for his efforts on behalf of the Club.

The Past Captains' Dinner 2006 and 2018

1951: the end of the debenture holders

At the end of his lengthy term as Chairman of Camden Place limited, H. Crewsdon Howard managed to persuade the long-suffering debenture holders to vote for their own extinction. An Extraordinary General Meeting was held on the evening of Saturday 10 November 1951. The directors and friends present plus proxies brought the voting strength that night to 58.5% which, according to schedule 4 of the original trust deed of 1899, was enough to constitute a quorum.

It was agreed that all debenture stock should be exchanged for shares, with £25 of debenture to be replaced by 499 one shilling shares, thereby increasing the nominal capital of the Company from £78 pounds to £3,600. Freed of prior charges on the property, the Board was now able to take a £10,000 mortgage with the Law Union and Rock and also to raise interest-free loans from selected members in return for lifetime exemption from the payment of their subscriptions.

White horses, red coats or Greek temple?

To celebrate the end of the debentures C.E. Fletcher presented the Club with its first flag and G.T. Shoosmith offered the flag staff from which it should fly. This flag generated considerable discussion as to what might be a suitable emblem for the Club.

Up until now the white horse of Kent, with its lower half bordered by the initials 'CGC' had been used for the buttons on the captains' redcoats and this design seems to have been the front-runner. But in the end the winning design of the Temple on a green background was adopted as the CGC symbol.

The logo was simplified and brought up to date in 2017.

The Temple Trophy

A.L.R. Hawkins, captain 1965, had the idea of getting a quote for a silver scale model of the Temple. The cost was £140 and the replica never leaves the clubhouse. It is played for annually in a foursomes match between the ladies and men.

Success on the course

As the Club and its members recovered from the war years, golfing success must have once more helped to raise spirits. 1947 saw Pat Jackson and his fellow team members decisively beat Knole Park by 7 ½ to 4 ½ to win the Perman Shield once more.

Chislehurst ladies also managed to maintain their success and profile, winning the Kent Golf Union Shield three more times in 1948, 1952 and 1959, whilst the Kent County continued to use CGC for some of their matches. Bridget Jackson picked up from where she had left off in 1939 with a string of successes and roles in county golf.

Ladies' golf is limited

Despite the fact that over the years ladies' golf at CGC had been such a strength, on Sunday 4 September 1949 at 5.30pm an EGM of the Club was suddenly called. The intention was to make an addition to Rule 38 determining that 'on Saturdays and Sundays, ladies playing together would give the courtesy of the course to men members on request'. The internal politics that prompted this action are now lost in time. General Meetings of the Club needed a quorum of ten and strangely nine good men were available to support their Captain G.P. Jackson on this occasion. Most of them had to be there for the Committee meeting scheduled at 6:00 p.m.

Despite this surprise restriction, the ladies at the Club continued to take a strong and active role, summed up by this extract from *Golf Illustrated* 8 December 1952. J.J.F. Pennink the Walker Cup player, laid it on the line when describing his visit to Camden place in 1952. *'the ladies ...... by no means take second place at Chislehurst.'*

1947
Chislehurst
wins Perman

1951
Debentures
extinguished

The late 50s and swinging 60s

During the 1950s and 1960s the Golf Club flag flew high in every sense. The members had billiards, tennis and squash for sport as well as golf; and the clubhouse was well used for social functions and bridge. The junior section was flourishing and was in such demand that for a while it became necessary to limit admission to the children of existing members. In the early days the men had looked after the juniors but once the numbers began to rise they very wisely deputised that task to the ladies. By 1966 the junior count was 85 boys and 27 girls.

Michael Attenborough

Learning his golf as a boy from Sydney Mason, Michael Attenborough showed early promise and became a boy international in 1957, having won the Kent Junior Championship in 1955 and 1956.

Over the next 30 plus years he won many competitions and played for England in internationals in 1964, 1966, 1967, and 1968. He played for the European team championship in 1967 and for Great Britain vs. Europe in 1966 to 1968 and versus America in the 1967 Walker Cup. He also won the President's Putter in 1962 and 1966. He retired from representative golf soon after that to concentrate on his career.

Although he played much of his golf at Royal St Georges, Sandwich, he remained a member of Chislehurst. He still found time to do his bit for CGC. He represented Chislehurst regularly for the Club's Perman and Kent Amateur Foursomes' teams and was a key member of the victorious teams of 1966 and 1967. He remained a very competitive player for a long time.

Michael was elected to the Club committee in 1968 and is credited with instigating the Men's Dinner Foursomes. He was Captain of Royal St Georges in 1982 and of the R&A in 1989/90 and he did us the honour of proposing the toast to the Captain and Club at the Men's Dinner in 1991. He is the current President of Royal St Georges.

Financial headaches continue

Whilst things on the course were going well, the directors of Camden Place Ltd. were not finding life so easy. Financial and staff problems dominated. Between 1958 and 1968 seven Club secretaries came and went, often with gaps between appointments. Domestic staff changed at monthly intervals and in 1963 Mrs Brem Wilson was heartily thanked for holding the fort as the sole cook in residence at the age of 83. Emmerson was making himself ill with overwork. Residents were still enjoying full board, seven days a week, including Christmas Day. The rate of £7 a week, already increased by 30%, was still not covering the costs. The further proposed price rise resulted in six rooms being vacant by June, with the subsequent loss of rental income

There was no longer a deposit account at Martin's Bank and the current account was permanently in deficit. In 1961 the Board flatly refused to contribute to the cost of setting up a permanent bar in the Faber lounge. The Committee went round the membership and suggested that the Club and Company might produce separate accounts in future. Such coolness between the two executive bodies of the Club was not productive.

Despite increases in membership, the Company's income always seemed inadequate to cover costs. The possibility of a dividend to shareholders was never even tabled. In 1962 with a total income of £16,272 the Company managed to declare a £446 profit but this was after spending as little as possible on the house and the course and allowing virtually nothing for depreciation.

1963 saw the end of both tennis and squash at the Club and some were concerned the golf would be the next to go.

Re-visiting the Club structure

In 1958 a joint working party of Board and Committee members agreed that the atmosphere at Camden Place would be much happier if all Club members held shares in the Company and every shareholder was a Golf Club member. An EGM in 1959 changed the Company's Articles slightly in order to allow this but gave no positive impetus towards its fulfilment.

Any real progress to such change would require the services of a dedicated individual with commitment, energy and talent. As Chairman of the Company Jack Stratford led from the front with the immediate purchase of more than 2,000 shares currently held by trustees. By November 1968 the Board was able to announce to the 69th AGM that Golf Club members now held a small majority among the registered owners of shares. This reduced the risks of decisions about the Club being in the hands of non-members.

Membership of both the Board and Committee was in practice by nomination. The Board had been accustomed to having at least one of its members on the Committee. In 1959 Roderick Travers Hawes tried hard to arrange some form of reciprocity but the best he could get from his colleagues was that

selected Committee members might be invited to sit in on Board meetings as observers.

A low point

In 1966 Jack Stratford stood down as Chairman in order to take over as Club Captain. His successor A.I. (Toddy) Todman took over an operation that was not doing well. There were vacancies for members and the house was under-let. Costs were going up, inflation was 3.7% and worse was to come. Selective Employment Tax was introduced that year putting the cost of employing staff up by 25 shillings a week per man, and 12s 6d per woman. Full-board residents added to these costs and the challenges of club management.

In 1967 the sterling crisis would lead to devaluation and the 70s were to be a hard decade for the country. The value of sterling against the dollar tumbled and in 1975 inflation hit 23.7%.

Despite these financial challenges there was still a general lack of commercial awareness at the Club; for example the summer ball, hailed a huge success, made a financial loss which the Company was asked to underwrite. The maximum income forecast for the year was £21,000.

Putting the house in order: the Toddy effect

Toddy's contribution to the Club was immense from the day he was elected. He was full of ideas. When asked where his inspiration came from he laughingly attributed it to his years at Sundridge Park. He had been refused membership of CGC in December 1937 and joined Sundridge Park instead!

On his appointment Toddy took action and started with reorganising the Board and then tackling the income shortfall. In 1967 the principle was established that the Captain should serve as a full director during his term of office. Each permanent director was entrusted with the supervision of a particular aspect of the Company's affairs.

House rents and club subscriptions were both increased by 20%, with the threat of more to come. The 30 guineas subscriptions would rise again to £45 by 1971. The cost of maintaining Camden Place with its listed building status was too much for the membership to bear so they were offered an alternative. As described in Section 1, the option of selling Camden Place and building a new clubhouse focused the members' minds and the complaints about

inconvenience and expense evaporated. It may cost the members money but they wanted to keep their iconic clubhouse.

By 1970 a subscription income of £12,414 was forecast and the Board decided to go to town on the ground floor, spending some £32,500 on improvements which were completed by the middle of 1971. J. Irons from Upminster Golf Club took over as Secretary in June 1970 whilst J. Bland and his wife took up residence in October 1972 as steward and cook. In 1973 Toddy was able to announce his retirement from the Board of a smoothly run company, now well in credit in its current account despite continuing losses on in-house catering.

1970
J. Irons appointed Secretary

1971
Golf subscriptions raised to £45 p.a.

The 70s and early 80s

The 70s began with Chislehurst at its best, showcasing great golf, supporting charity and celebrating its history.

Bernard Gallacher and Peter Oosterhuis

In May 1970, Dr Ian Kelsey-Fry (Captain 1969) organized a grand exhibition match in aid of charity. The idea was that two top-class amateurs Michael Bonallack and Michael Attenborough should play with two promising young professionals. Bonallack would be rewarded with honorary membership of Chislehurst and the professionals would each receive a small fee.

Michael Attenborough came to the rescue when Bonallack fell ill at the last moment. He drove to the members' bar at Sunningdale and recruited Michael Burgess, another English international. The professionals were Bernard Gallacher and Peter Oosterhuis, both Attenborough acquaintances.

On a very wet day, Oosterhuis and Burgess won in a well-supported event, generating £253. 11s for the charity Multiple Sclerosis. As Oosterhuis addressed the ball on 18th tee, Gallagher offered a stage whisper to the effect 'this for a 59', a score which was unheard of in those days; and this was despite the fact that Oosterhuis had driven out of bounds at the 11th!

NAPOLEON III
EMPEREUR DES FRANCAIS
VECUT A CAMDEN PLACE DE 1871 A 1873
IL Y MOURUT LE 9 JANVIER 1873
L'IMPERATRICE EUGENIE Y VECUT DE 1870 A 1881
LE PRINCE IMPERIAL Y VECUT DE 1870 A 1879
IL MOURUT HEROIQUEMENT EN AFRIQUE DU SUD
SOUS L'UNIFORME BRITANNIQUE

Napoleon and Eugénie remembered

The centenary of Empress Eugénie's arrival at Camden Place with the Prince Imperial was on 20 September 1970. To mark the occasion Prince Louis Murat led a pilgrimage of enthusiastic Frenchmen to Chislehurst and Woolwich. Mass was celebrated at St Mary's, presided over by the Archbishop of Southwark, followed by a gathering at the Prince Imperial Monument and then a buffet lunch at Camden Place.

Some 28 months later in January 1973 a much larger party visited to mark the centenary of Napoleon lll's death. Toddy Todman addressed a huge gathering in the mixed lounge. To commemorate the occasion the Club was presented with the plaque that now adorns the front of the clubhouse, to the left of the main doorway. It was installed and formally unveiled in December 1974 by Count Walewski, President of The Friends of Napoleon lll – Historical Society.

A new Professional: David Pratt (1974-1978)

Sydney Mason retired in 1974. His successor was David Pratt. He had won the Kent Assistants' Championship during his time at Shooters Hill and he arrived with some new ideas and it was good to have a playing professional; Mason had not played since the late 1930's. Pratt introduced the Captain/ Professional matches which have continued ever since. He also used his playing connections to stage a couple of exhibition matches. In the first he played with Carole Radford, Nick Job and Michael Attenborough (who shot a 64). The second match featured Henry Cooper, George Will and Danny Blanchflower. David Pratt left in 1978.

Subscriptions increased

The 70's started with subscription rates of £45 for the men and £30 for the ladies. The Board was reluctant to accept the inevitability of annual increases in these rates but was convinced by 1976, following several years of rapid inflation.

Chislehurst had operated a generous pricing strategy which arose in part because of the Board's stated policy that subscriptions should cover the wages and salaries bill (and no more). This approach left the Company chronically short of cash for any sort of capital expenditure. All old-age pensioners benefited from a discount of 25% and the young also had concessions. With a growing number of five day members (87 men and 43 ladies by 1980) paying 5/7ths of the full-day membership (plus their pensioner discount) golf at Chislehurst was relatively cheap. An aging playing membership meant golf-subscription income could be expected to fall.

The inevitable happened. By 1980 subscriptions had risen to £140 plus VAT for men and £110 for ladies. Quite an increase in ten years.

Catering becomes a franchise

The economic conditions continued to be challenging and managing a listed building complete with demanding residents did not get any easier. By 1977 the forecast loss on catering reached £8,000. Changes were needed. Arrangements were made for the catering to be let out as a franchise. Looking back on that time, 15 years after his retirement, Secretary J. Irons said *'If only it could have happened sooner it would have saved me a great deal of trouble and heartache and a lot of money for the club'*.

More members held shares

Chislehurst was not yet entirely a members club but by now 75% of the company shares were in the names of Golf Club members.

1974
Captain/Pro challenge matches start

1974
David Pratt appointed Club Professional

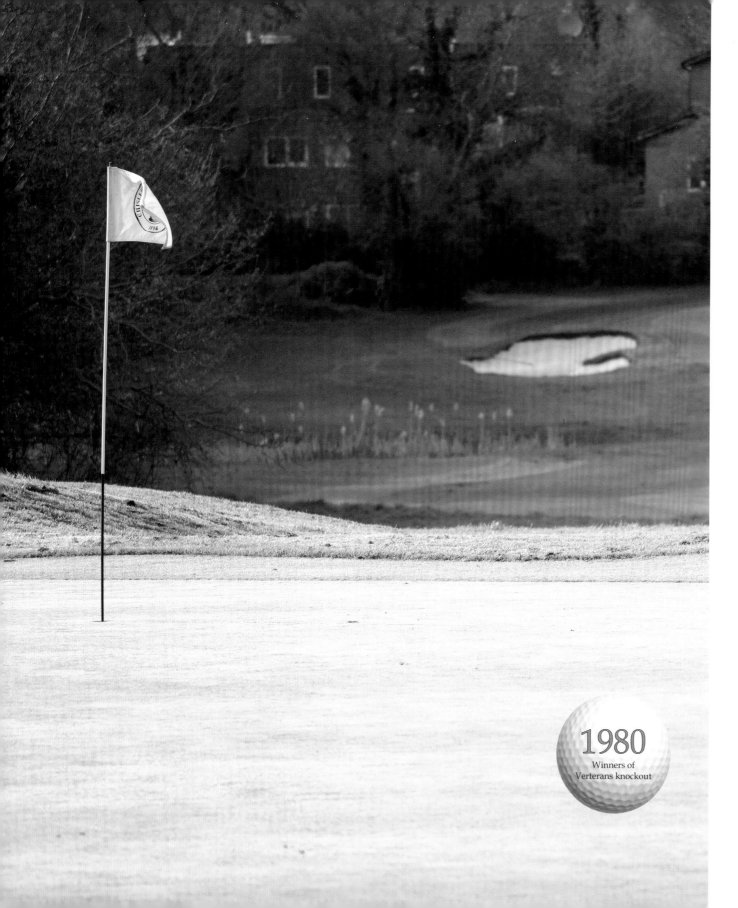

Establishing the T's & T's

Out on the course, established golfers who had retired from work found themselves outnumbered by the rising tide of midweek members. The custom developed that fours should not be organized in advance on Tuesdays and Thursdays but made up in order of arrival at the clubhouse. J. Crabb took on the role of unofficial marshal.

In 1977 Chislehurst linked up with Royal Blackheath and some others to found Group 2 of the Kent County Veterans League, first set up four years previously by the Society of Kent Golf Club Veterans. K. S. Ryle became the manager of the Veterans League team. Their results in the league were always respectable and they managed to win the Veterans knockout in 1980. This involved a wider selection of clubs from all over Kent and gave rise to lasting connections with Littlestone and Royal Cinque Ports.

1980
Winners of
Verterans knockout

Kent Veterans winnners 1980

Golfing notes

Whilst social golf was clearly flourishing at home, Club members were not making much of a mark in open competition in the 70s. The Perman team was wallowing in the depths of a 23 year gap between finals. However P.J.H. Daubney managed to equal the course record. His many appearances on the honours boards in the clubhouse extend from the Victory Cup in 1959 to a sixth scratch medal in 1984.

The Club was producing some wonderful juniors but their time was yet to come and the old guard were past their prime. The mixture had its moments. In 1976 for example CGC was drawn away against an extremely strong Sundridge Park team which included Jeremy Smith. Jeremy, another successful product of the Mason teaching school, had chosen to represent Sundridge Park to further his county ambitions, although he always retained his Chislehurst membership. Jeremy's brother Trevor was in the Chislehurst team, which was not expected to win more than a couple

of points. CGC won the foursomes 3–1. In the singles Michael Attenborough beat Jeremy Smith 4 and 3 and Chislehurst won the match. The ladies also had their successes. In 1973 they won the Holland Trophy, a foursome event for handicaps of 12 or less. Mrs Hildegard Stacey replaced Mrs Patricia Gooda as a partner for Mrs Noble after the first two rounds and took a full share in the defeat of Littlestone in the final by 7 and 5.

John Kelsey-Fry played for the Perman

team in 1973 at the age of 16 and was the Club's first junior to be given a new status so that he could play in adult competitions. David Rutnam (Captain 1992), was the third to be given this status and he first played Perman golf in 1975 also as a 16-year-old. David Theobald surpassed them both when he played at the age of 15 in 1979. John Kelsey-Fry went on to win the Kent Cob at Knole Park in 1979.

Henry Turner

The men established a scratch knockout competition in 1971 and Henry Turner donated the trophy despite a committee recommendation that the money might more suitably be spent on a practice net. The first winner was P.J.H. Daubney.

Henry Turner was not a single figure golfer himself. Well known at Lloyd's and as often as not dressed in business attire, Henry was accustomed to descend with great dignity from his upstairs residence in Camden Place and play the perfect host to any midweek societies whose members looked a little lost.

A famous Club story describes how in the course of their annual fixture against the Club, the Band of Brothers wished to do the honours after lunch, only to find that the steward had run out of kummel. Though not himself involved in the match, Henry immediately sprang to the rescue: *'I always keep four bottles under my bed in case of emergency!'*

Turner Trophy

Wilding Cole Team 1981

Improving golf

After the rather inward-looking 1970s, the 1980s present an altogether brighter picture at the Club. Monthly medals started being played in threes and on a single day. This enhanced their merit as a competitive test of golf and encouraged much wider participation by the membership. The conversion of the Faber lounge for use as a spike bar was an immediate success and by 1979 a new Secretary lived over the shop.

N.E. Pearson: Club Secretary (1979-2001)

Nigel Edwin (Gunner) Pearson joined the Club as Secretary in 1979. He was well organised and helped the Club develop through the 80s and 90s. He joined after leaving his beloved Ndola Golf Club, Zambia where he had been their Captain for two consecutive years and then their Secretary. He may not have expected it when he was appointed but he was a moderniser for our Club, which maybe needed a nudge.

Nigel was particularly supportive of the juniors, the various club teams, greyhound racing, Charlton Athletic, Senior Service cigarettes and occasionally Gordon's gin! Through Nigel's influence, enthusiasm and general love of the game of golf, the playing side of the Club suddenly became better supported, more successful and most importantly more enjoyable.

He was responsible for three new golf events on the calendar.

Firstly, supported by the ladies, he set up the Junior Open for which he provided the handicap cup. David Theobald Senior presented the scratch cup.

His second initiative was The Chislehurst Salvers. It started in 1990 and is an annual four-cornered match between Chislehurst, Royal Blackheath, Langley Park and Knole Park. As would be expected it is competitive but fun, played by seven pairs in handicap groups. It has been fantastically successful ever since.

The third inspiration was the Secretary's Day, traditionally played on the August Bank Holiday Monday, now rebadged as the General Manager's Day.

In his prime Nigel was a golfer with a unique style off a competitive 7 handicap, a cricketer of some competence and a hockey player; all of which meant he was interested in playing hard and celebrating success and failure in time-honoured ways. It was no great surprise that the men's section won 13 of the Association of South Eastern Golf Club trophies in his 22 years, compared with 3 in the previous 22 years. At the same time he nurtured a crop of youngsters who also won several trophies and of whom the Club could be justly proud. It may not all be down to the Gunner but he was certainly a catalyst.

Chislehurst Salvers Team 1991

More tournaments

The institution of the Brothers Open Tournament in 1979 was a great personal achievement of that year's Captain, P. W. S. Boult. In 1980 came the first Chislehurst Junior Open Day. Held on a Wednesday in August, the Junior Open has been successful from the start. It had been requested in an entry in the suggestion book dated 6 March 1979 signed by seven juniors headed by P.J. Foord, later to be Club Secretary from 2003 – 2008. In 1981 the age limit for the Junior Open was increased to 19 and the number of holes to 36. For the first three years the winner was David J. Theobald.

Wilding Cole Trophy Team 1988

1979
The Brothers Open begins

1980
Junior Open begins

David Theobald

David Theobald captained Kent under 18s and under 21s. He had already played for the Perman Shield team at the tender age of 15 before he won the first three Junior Opens at Chislehurst. In 1981 he managed to win six junior open competitions in Kent. He also won the 1981 Daily Express National at La Manga. Besides his individual successes he played his part in helping Chislehurst to win the Kent Junior Inter-Club Championship in 1981.

David was runner-up in the Kent Amateur Championship in 1987 and also played in Open Championship final qualifiers on three different occasions. Back at Chislehurst he famously captained the enormously successful Perman Shield and Kent Foursomes teams in 1999 and 2000.

A winning streak

Chislehurst had not really been a competitive force at inter-club level for some years, and certainly not at the handicap levels above the scratch requirements of the Perman Shield team. Only twice had our Club's name been engraved on any of the other trophies on offer through the Association of South Eastern Golf Clubs.

In the 80s things changed. The Club won no less than six of those competitions, starting in 1981 with a famous win in the final of the Wilding Cole Trophy (handicap 9 and over) against Wildernesse G.C. The team selected was a blend of youth and experience, managed by M.M. Freeman, and it waltzed to a comfortable victory. The Club Captain, Robin Furniss, returned to Camden Place with an elated team who partied well into the early hours. Indeed the Captain got his wife out of bed at about midnight (they lived beside the 3rd green) to join in the celebrations. It signalled the start of Chislehurst becoming competitive at all levels and set the bar in how to celebrate those victories.

Next came back-to-back wins in the Gray Cup (handicaps 18 and over) in 1983 and 1984. The Wilding Cole was won again in 1986, 1988 and in 1995. Interleaving these wins were victories in the Royal Blackheath Trophy in 1989 (handicaps 15 and over) and our solitary win in the Sundridge Park trophy in 1994 (handicaps 6 and over).

The ladies were adding their successes to the CGC tally, winning the Kent Division of the Pearson Trophy in 1981 and 1988.

Our inter-club trophies

The Association of South Eastern Golf Clubs is administered from Royal Blackheath. It is an extension of the eight original clubs which played for the Perman Shield from 1925 and now comprises 16 clubs. Trophies for different handicap groups were added over time; the Sundridge Park Trophy 1978 (6+ handicap), Wilding Cole trophy 1935 (9+), West Kent trophy 1970 (12+), Royal Blackheath trophy 1955 (15+) and Gray Cup 1972 (18+). (These handicap levels were subsequently amended.)

Pearson Trophy Team 1981

In addition the ladies won the Kent Golf Union Shield on eight occasions, five before WWll and three more times before 1960.

Year	Team Victories before the Centenary
1923	London Amateur Foursomes
1924	London Amateur Foursomes
1928	London Amateur Foursomes
1929	Perman Shield
1930	Perman Shield
1938	Perman Shield
1938	London Amateur Foursomes
1947	Perman Shield
1957	Wilding Cole
1963	Royal Blackheath Trophy
1966	Perman Shield
1967	Kent Foursomes
1980	Kent Veterans
1981	Pearson Trophy Kent Division
1981	Wilding Cole
1981	Knole Park Junior Trophy
1983	Gray Cup
1984	Gray Cup
1986	Wilding Cole
1988	Wilding Cole
1988	Pearson Trophy Kent Division
1989	Royal Blackheath Trophy
1991	Knole Park Junior Trophy

Standing guard over the silver shield that has been returned to Camden Place are soldiers of the Kings Troop, Royal Artillery. Also pictured are Chislehurst Golf Club members Captain and Mrs Furniss, ladies captain Mrs C. T. Stacey and family and footman Mr Culver.

Glittering gala recreates Camden's colourful past

An Imperial celebration

One further social occasion was held in honour of our links the Imperial Family. It was to belatedly mark the centenary of The Prince Imperial's death that R.H. Furniss and Mrs H. Stacey (Captain and Lady Captain) held a function at Camden Place in September 1981.

Bill Mitchell described the event: *'They assembled an impressive display of Napoleonic memorabilia, including the shield which Eugénie had donated to the mess at Woolwich in 1880 as a memento of her son's close links with the Academy and the regiment. Next door in the mixed lounge the RA orchestra gave two performances, and a beefeater stood guard in the billiard room over a full set of the crown jewels in replica'*. It must have been quite splendid.

Imperial Shield © Kentish Times

A GLITTERING spectacle of music and tradition lit up Camden Place, Chislehurst, last Saturday, to celebrate its historic past.

Once the home of Emperor Napoleon III, and now the headquarters of Chislehurst Golf Club, Camden played host for the commemorative evening, recreating the atmosphere of the 1880's.

Responsible for organising the gala was Mrs Hilda Stacey — the golf club's ladies' captain. "Months of preparation went into this and lots of hard work — Hilda has really pulled off an amazing event," said men's captain Mr Robin Furniss.

Footmen in period costume greeted the guests and trumpeters from the Kings Troop Royal Artillery blew ceremonial fanfares.

An exhibition called "Historic Camden Place", was mounted by Mr Ken Wilson, but pride of place went to a shimmering silver shield guarded by soldiers from the Kings Troop, which had returned to Camden for the first time in 100 years.

CLOSE LINKS

The shield was taken from Camden Place in 1880 when Empress Eugene presented it to the Royal Artillery Officer's Mess at Woolwich.

"The club has close links with the Royal Artillery and many of our senior members are ex-gunners," said Mr Furniss.

The immediate past captain of the club, Colonel Reg Pont, brought the shield from Woolwich along with a full replica set of the Crown jewels.

The evening was completed by music from the Royal Artillery orchestra and a firework display.

Glittering celebration

A GLITTERING evening of history and music was enjoyed by around 100 guests at a special centenary occasion at Camden Place, the celebrated former home of Napoleon III and present home of Chislehurst Golf Club, last Saturday.

Highlight of the evening was the arrival of the Empress Eugenie Shield returned to Chislehurst from the Royal Artillery officer's mess in Woolwich after more than 100 years. Full story and picture page 11.

(V/40918/3A)

Admiring a replica set of Crown Jewels at the Camden Place celebration evening are Mrs Doreen Marle and her daughter Liza.

WARNING
DEEP WATER

The 80s and 90s

I n 1982 P. D. Gibson became Captain. There followed a series of decisions which demonstrated the management skills which he would display as Chairman of the Company from 1985 to 1991.

Numbers and newts

The maximum numbers allowed for seven-day membership were reduced to 310 for men and 120 for ladies. It was accepted that many five-day members had no wish for anything more. Their maximum numbers were now set at 90 and 40. Another 25 who aspired to full membership but had not yet an adequate handicap, were to be allowed limited access to the course at weekends to help them on their way. Transferring the ladies' medal to Wednesday allowed Thursday to become the principal day for 36–hole societies. The veterans could beaver away from the 10th on Tuesdays and Thursdays without distraction.

Small matters got just the same attention as great. On Monday 6 December at the committee meeting during which the new membership limits had been agreed, the clock stood 10:18 pm by the time the 22nd item on the agenda was introduced: 'disturbance by golfers to great crested newts' who tended to conduct their courting near the ponds on the 1st and 15th holes. After full consideration, two decisions were reached. A courteous letter of comfort should be sent to the British Herpetological Society and appropriate action should be taken on the course by G.P.H. Grenfell and his green committee. The newts have not left.

The London Ladies Foursomes

In 1983 the London Ladies Foursomes made a sentimental journey back to Chislehurst after an interval of 61 years. Fifty pairs competed. The course was in good condition but the weather was terrible. On the final day the Secretary and his gallant troop of past captains and juniors did yeoman service to keep the greens puddle free. The home club represented by Miss Brenda Gibson and Mrs P. Giddins played very well to reach the quarter-final, which they lost to the ultimate winners

1983
the Artisans retire

The end of the Artisans

Set up by Sydney Mason in 1938, the Artisans enjoyed golf for a nominal fee in exchange for work on the course. They had a marvellous run of 30 years but by the 1970s they had become something of an anachronism. In 1973 C. H. T. Garner's committee of inquiry came up with the unanimous recommendation *'that the artisan section should be phased out over a period of three years – by 1st January 1977'*. The period of notice was generous but successive captains blanched at the very thought of broaching such an issue with John Dorrell, the Artisan's respected Secretary. It was therefore not until 1982 that the nettle was finally grasped. John Dorrell had now retired; all past captains were consulted and on the 15 May P. D. Gibson felt able to inform the 69 members present to the AGM that the Artisan's would fade away at the end of May 1983.

Professional changes

The 80s and 90s also saw changes in the Professional's shop. David Pratt was followed by Keith MacDonald in 1978. His father was Professional at The Berkshire and had once led The Open. Keith was plagued by back problems during his time at Chislehurst. He was still good enough to make the final qualifier at North Foreland for the 1981 Open Championship. He left for Goodwood GC and his back problems seemed to ease somewhat. He is still the course record holder at Mid Kent Golf Club, where he had a putt for a 59, before settling for a 60. He played for a couple of years very successfully on the Seniors' Tour before he needed hip replacement surgery and died suddenly from a blood clot at the age of 53.

MacDonald was followed by Andrew Thompson in 1982. He joined us from Eltham Warren Golf Club. He reached the Open Championship final qualifier in 1985. However the pressures of a young family and an ambition to run his own golf school led Andrew to leave in 1988 and set up a new facility, Otter Valley Golf Centre near Exeter.

Stewart Corstorphine followed and he stayed until 1993. He was a genial big-hitting Scot and a good teacher but he needed wider fairways than were on offer at Chislehurst!

Mark Lawrence, a junior at Chislehurst in his early years who went on to win three Kent Amateur Championships, returned to the Club as Professional in 1993. He was a very fine golfer but retired in 2001 to help his father's shipping business.

Mike Collett and Professional Mark Lawrence at the 1995 Captains' Drive In with Nigel Pearson in attendance.

Changes to the ladies' course

In 1985 the LGU ruled that Category A golfers needed a Standard Scratch Score of at least 70 for handicap purposes. Chislehurst's SSS was 68. Yardage increases of 123 yards were needed to raise the SSS to the required level. At the ladies' AGM in autumn of the same year new tee arrangements were agreed to allow the necessary increases to the SSS. Jeanne Gibson's course record of 67 in July 1985 was therefore consigned to the history books because of the re-measured course and Pauline Giddins took that mantle with a 71 in October 86. Golf is silly sometimes! Jeanne Gibson married, moved up north and in 1990 broke the ladies course record at Hoylake, John Dun's home course, where she scored a 69 (5 under par) whilst she was five months pregnant.

Surprisingly the LGU revoked their 1985 decision only six years later.

...and the Club structure

When asked about his time as Chairman, Michael Hollingsworth (1998–2004) started by highlighting the importance of Peter Gibson's contribution as Chairman in establishing the foundations that ensured the future of the Club. 'He re-organised the structure of the Company so that it was totally in the control of the Golf Club membership as shareholders. He had also instigated administrative reform by establishing sub-committees of the Board, each chaired by a Director.' This was a key time in the development of a more modern club.

Never trust a weather forecast

On the night of 15 October 1987, despite reassurances from weather forecaster Michael Fish, one of the strongest UK storms ever recorded passed over Kent. It left 22 people dead and the UK insurance industry facing £1.4bn in claims. Over 15 million trees were blown down, power lines destroyed, roads and railway lines blocked and ships capsized. Kent was badly affected. Sevenoaks lost six of its famous seven! CGC got off more lightly than many but still lost a number of trees, the most significant being some of Weston's original avenue of lime trees that graced the entrance driveway.

1987
Weston's avenue of trees
damaged

Some storms don't blow over

There was one unfortunate incident at the Club in the late 80s which has gone down in the annals of the Club history. The Chislehurst police, P Division, got into the habit of visiting the Club late evenings 'to check on security'. Being hospitable, the officers concerned would be offered refreshment. On one occasion the bar manager opened the bar and served two of the Metropolitan Police's finest a couple of drinks.

For reasons that we will never know, said bar manager then went outside and got into the squad car and drove it off down the driveway. One problem...... the bar manager could not drive! The inevitable outcome was a written-off police car and a damaged tree in the driveway. The bar manager was prosecuted, whilst the policemen had a lot of explaining to do back at the station (which today is a restaurant).

Ladies get the vote

Eventually in 1992 the club rules were amended to give ladies the vote at the Golf Club AGM. The Men's Captain is now elected at the AGM, usually a few days prior to the Men's Dinner, rather than at an EGM during the dinner as had been the custom.

The Men's Dinner

The ceremony to install the new captain, marked by him changing into his red jacket, is still retained as the high point of a busy Men's Dinner evening. Starting with a draw for the Dinner Foursomes played the following morning, it continues on to speculative investment in the outcome of these foursomes and in the power and accuracy of the incoming Captain's drive. It is followed by the dinner itself, with the departing Captain's swan song.

With so much entertainment provided other hijinks have become lost in the mists of time. No vehicle has made it inside the central hall for a decade or three. It is longer still since the last motorcycle was ridden up the stairs, although there has been some 'bobsleigh' racing down them. Bleary eyed golfers, still in dinner jackets, are still a common sight at the start of the men's foursomes on the Saturday morning.

The Captain's Jewel

In 1989 Brig. F. Pocock OBE MC (Captain 1962) designed and made the Captain's Jewel when he was over 90 years old. The front has as its centrepiece a beautiful Napoleon coin. The reverse has an engraving of the Temple. Crossed golf clubs attach it to a green ribbon. The first captain to wear it was W. J. Marle in 1990.

Captain Bill Edwards (2012) with the winning Royal Blackheath Trophy team

Captain David Hatton (2004) and incoming Captain David Smith with the Imperial Shield on loan for the evening

Towards the Millennium

The Club was so lucky to have the effervescent Norman Dyer and Jenny Kerr as Captains in the centenary year, expertly supported by the Centenary Committee headed by Michael Hollingsworth and the social side led by Ken Stone. It did not start perfectly for Norman, whose tee shot at his drive-in actually came to rest left of the Temple! But that was just the start of the fun, led by a Captain who affectionately became known as 'Champagne Charlie'.

'The Club celebrated its centenary over a two-week period. The weather was glorious and there were two main events on the programme, the Ball and Family Fun Day. The Ball proceedings began with a great surprise! The Royal Artillery Marching Band, hidden in Camden Park Road, crested the 14th playing stirring, triumphant pieces as they approached the clubhouse. They were greeted by a huge crowd to rapturous applause and entertained them into the night with their 12–piece band.'

Ken Stone

The Royal Artillery Marching Band preparing to open the Centenary Ball.

Celebrating the centenary

The Family Fun Day was a huge success on a glorious July day. Overflow parking required us to open the 9th fairway which filled to capacity. The revellers enjoyed side-shows and stalls, food, drink and entertainment. Skydivers from Headcorn Aerodrome came gliding down, successfully landing on the 14th cross bunker as planned, to great applause.

We were taken back to 1894 by a group of Vintage Golfers, attired in period clothing using traditional equipment, who played the last four holes. Juniors caddied, others acting as ball spotters all dressed as urchins, their faces smeared with dirt! The dress code was definitely relaxed that day. A massive crowd followed the matches around, with one player saying they had never performed to such a large audience. For the record one of their number finished 1 under par!

It was a magnificent day enjoyed by all and a fitting end to a wonderful two weeks showing off Chislehurst Golf Club at its best.'

As a postscript to this, there was a very successful 'Costume 1894' evening in October, when the choir of the Chislehurst Police Station (which had been opened in 1893) sang a spirited rendition of 'Champagne Charlie', so perhaps they had by then forgotten the squad car incident of the late 80s.

Arriving at the ball in style

Winners of the Centenary Pro-Am

The Centenary Ball programme signed by the attendant past captains. Dad was Dr. M. Hatton.

Of course there were also centenary golfing events:

- A Centenary Pro-Am won by D. C. Theobald, I. J. Coombs and N. E. Pearson, with professional Simon Wood.

- A triangular match with Dulwich & Sydenham GC and Purley Downs GC, both of whom were also celebrating their centenary. Mixed teams of 20 played simultaneously on each course…................... Chislehurst came third!

- An invitation meeting was held for current Kent Captains and Lady Captains.

- The Centenary Medal was added to the golfing diary.

- Reflecting Camden Place's historic connections with Compiègne, men's and ladies' teams from Compiègne GC played at the Club following very successful home and away fixtures from the previous year.

An old cup returns

A.L.R. (Tony) Hawkins (Captain 1965 and Chairman 1995 to 1998) was a very knowledgeable and enthusiastic collector of golf memorabilia. Somehow he found, bought and returned the cup which was presented by A.N. Lubbock as his Captains Prize in 1914 and won by H. F. White. Simon Wright was the first recipient in 1996 and it is now presented annually to the winner of the Captain's Prize.

A golf anniversary

One other anniversary was celebrated before the millennium. In 1998 the 50th match was played against Honourable Artillery Company who presented CGC with a print of Armoury House, their most impressive HQ hidden amongst the offices near Old Street, London EC1.

Peter Downs had taken over as Chairman in 1991, building on the Gibson approach, but following his death in 1995 Tony Hawkins succeeded to the Chair. He also continued the same policies but he had to resign on health grounds in 1998.

The 1980s and 90s had seen an increase in the supply of golf facilities as some landowners turned fields into golf courses, whilst corporate brands consolidated groups of courses under an umbrella of connected facilities. This increased competition was changing expectations of what the modern golfer wanted from their club. Despite this Chislehurst was basking in a wave of success.

Eight glorious years

In inter-club competitions Chislehurst enjoyed a purple patch, winning 11 team events from the centenary in 1994 to 2002. In those eight years CGC won each of the five handicap levels of the Men's Association of South Eastern Golf Club at least once. To this impressive total can be added wins in the Veterans league, a ladies KCLGA knock-out competition and three junior team trophies. This run of victories was crowned by winning the big prize, the Perman Shield two years running!

Team Victories post centenary	Year	Team Captain
Sundridge Park Trophy	1994	J. E. A. Walker
Junior Inter-Club Trophy	1994	R. Moger
Wilding Cole Trophy	1995	N. E. Pearson
Gray Cup	1996	F. R. Burnett
Knole Park Junior Trophy	1996	D. C. Keenan
Blackheath Trophy	1997	N. J. Dyer
West Kent Trophy	1999	I. Herrington
Perman Shield	1999	D. C. Theobald
Perman Shield	2000	D. C. Theobald
Kent Foursomes	2000	D. C. Theoblad
Blackheath Trophy	2001	P. J. Foord
Vets InterClub Cup	2001	R.C. Purkiss
Knole Park Junior Trophy	2001	C..Aked
Coombe Cup	2002	Mrs B. Hatton & Mrs G. Evans
Blackheath Trophy	2004	P. J. Stevenson
Vets InterClub Cup	2004	F.R. Burnett
West Kent Trophy	2005	D. Spragg
Ladies Business League	2007	Ms S. Smollett
Ladies Business League	2008	Ms S. Smollett
Blackheath Trophy	2012	C. Chandler
Srixon Junior Foursomes	2013	E. Holmans
West Kent Trophy	2014	P. G. Matthews
Knole Park Junior Trophy	2015	A. Willsmer
Langley Park Youth League	2016	T. Andrews
Ladies Business League	2016	Ms J. Russell
Lohan Trophy	2016	Ms J. Lamb & Ms.J Buckland
Shooters Hill Youth Cup	2017	M. Wen

It is impossible to detail all the individual contributions and celebrations following those wonderful afternoons, but a few are worthy of mention:

- Danny Winter halved his match in the final of the 1995 Wilding Cole by holing in one at Langley Park's 18th hole, part of a 6–2 victory

- The Club's West Kent Trophy side beat Sidcup at Wrotham Heath in pitch darkness in 2005, the 18th being played by the last pairing under the lights from the clubhouse and the headlights of several cars, orchestrated by team captain David Spragg and his torch.

- The Coombe Cup is a Kent County LGA foursomes KO competition for ladies over 68 years old, started in 1995. The entry in 2002 was 84 teams!

- The Lohan Trophy is another Kent County LGU matchplay foursomes knock out, with pairs comprising one adult and one junior member. Jo Lamb and Joely Buckland beat Nizels GC in the final at Ashford GC.

Winners of the Ladies Business League 2007

133

Junior winners of the Knowle Park Trophy 2015

Return of the Perman Shield and Kent Foursomes

After 33 years the Perman Shield returned to Chislehurst. CGC had lost rather one-sided finals to Sundridge Park in 1989 and then to Knole Park in 1997 but things were changing.

In 1999 the team, led by the inventive and inspirational David Theobald, beat Wrotham Heath on a countback in the semi-final and met the multiple winners Sundridge Park in the final at Royal Blackheath. CGC were 1–3 down in the morning foursomes but came back with a 5–3 singles win and an overall match score of 6–6. Countback! The Sundridge Park captain thought they had won but was soon corrected by Peter Foord and Chislehurst won by one hole. It was such a close match it is difficult to point to any game-changing moments, but Jeremy Smith's 7th hole miracle was perhaps just that. His tee shot was wild and lost; three off the tee and then 160 yards to go....which he proceeded to hole! Ross Galgutt's 6 & 4 win was just as worthy of a headline.

The Kent Foursomes team of 1999 nearly repeated the Perman success at Sundridge Park, eventually losing the final to Wrotham Heath at the first extra hole.

Lightning struck again the following year when Chislehurst retained the Perman Shield, again beating Sundridge Park in the final, this time at Rochester & Cobham. Again CGC came back for a 1–3 deficit at lunch to win the singles 6–2 without losing any match (4 wins, 4 halves).

More drama followed when Chislehurst won the Kent Foursomes for the first time

Kent Amateaur Foursomes 2000

since 1967 at Wrotham Heath. And amazingly it was Sundridge Park who were again the opponents. The Sundridge Park pair of McNamara and Brosnan managed to birdie the 17th and 18th to take the match to sudden death and then birdied the 19th as well but Simon Wright and Ross Galgutt also birdied four of the last five holes. To cap it off Wright holed for an eagle at the first extra hole to complete an historic triumph.

The noughties

In 1998 Michael Hollingsworth was appointed Chairman. He recalled *'As we entered the new millennium, changes were afoot. For example modern technology enabled us to introduce the 'swipe card', initially for a secure entry system but soon it was extended to cover payments for food and drink. Social change was also evident. The formality of previous generations had been eroded and there were and will continue to be knock-on effects on the values and traditions of an established members' club.'*

The Hollingsworth Board was able to sanction expenditure on the house especially the public rooms. Attention was paid to consolidating the company's financial position, focusing on the need to increase membership as the principal source of revenue as well as marketing the Club's facilities. Their work meant the scene was set for those following on during the remainder of the noughties and beyond to carry the Club forward.

Lady Captain's Day 1997

Equal status for the ladies

A most notable and well overdue change was the parity of playing rights for all adult full-playing members. In 2001 our alcohol licence again came under some pressure. At that time a Club Licence lasted ten years but the local courts let it be known that the licence would be at risk if the practice of restricted playing rights for ladies at weekends, and for which they paid slightly less, was not addressed.

One local club tested the courts and it resulted in a licence that was not renewed for several months! It should not have been a major issue for CGC, since the AGM in 1997 had already established that business ladies should be able to play at weekends without restrictions and they had an intermediate subscription category. The Captain of the day, Andrew Keenan, skilfully managed a packed AGM that changed the rules and protected the licence. The restrictions to playing times disappeared, and any difference in subscription was phased out.

135

CGC changes Rose's luck?

Rose had famously missed 21 consecutive cuts in a row after turning professional in 1998. After he played at Chislehurst his fortunes changed somewhat and by 2018 he had won 25 titles worldwide, plus the US Open in 2013 and the Gold Medal at the 2016 Olympics in Rio de Janeiro. In 2018 he reached number one in the world rankings.

2001
Justin Rose
plays Chislehurst

Justin Rose

Staff changes

Nigel Pearson's 22 year tenure as Secretary finished when he retired in November 2001 but not before a most enjoyable party and an exhibition 9 holes from Justin Rose, Andrew Butterfield and Scott Stevens (the latter two having been assistant professionals attached to Chislehurst).

Nigel was succeeded by David Bowles, who was then replaced in early 2003, when Peter Foord was appointed. Peter had been a member for some 30 years since the age of nine and proved a successful administrator, until he was also lured away by Royal Mid Surrey.

On the course Gary Tait gave way to Peter Gee in January 2003. This was a departure from the Club's past employment approach. Rather than rely on internal promotion the Board chose to hire a professionally qualified head greenkeeper.

Apart from those changes on the course and in the Office, there were also changes in the Professional's shop with the appointment of Jonathan Bird and in the kitchen where, following the departure of Craig Frith, Leon and Doreen de Bruyn took on the franchise. Sadly, Doreen died quite suddenly but Leon continued to feed the Club for some years.

2003
the Club appoints the first professional Head Greenkeeper

Unsung heroes

A special mention must be given to Maureen Finlay, whose cheerful 16-year stint in the office ended in February 2003 when she retired.

Likewise Anne Wren, who would retire in March 2015, completed nearly 25 years of service. It would be difficult to describe everything these ladies did. Suffice it to say they did everything that the Secretary did not!

David Emmerson, son of Leslie Thomas Emmerson, retired from the Club in 2004 after ten years of service, finally ending a long and wonderful association with that family.

The Club owes them a great debt of gratitude.

Maureen Finlay with her son Robert during his Captaincy year 2018

Changes at the top

Michael Hollingsworth stepped down as Chairman after six years and was replaced by J.M.B. Lenton in November 2004. The Lenton Board was determined from an early stage to protect the membership from significant subscription increases by looking at improving externally generated income, mainly from profitable use of the clubhouse. It was expected that this would then help reduce the impact on members of the ongoing need for major capital and maintenance expenditure.

John Lenton explained the Board's strategy. *'We looked carefully at income generation as a Board and recognised the need to upgrade the quality of the outside function offering at the Club. To this end, and driven by Gary Wilson, the marketing of the clubhouse, particularly for weddings, was completely changed. The offering was upgraded considerably. We gained a licence to hold wedding*

ceremonies and a House Manager (Ian Trotter) was employed. Income from outside functions increased substantially, taking some pressure off increases in members' subscriptions.'

Unfortunately this vision was frustrated as CGC faced the wider implications of the banking collapse of 2007/8 and its impact on the economy. It was a catalyst that led to the loss of a number of courses in the following years, including Deangate Ridge, Austen Lodge, Broke Hill, Beckenham Place Park, Cranbrook (formerly Hemsted Forest) and Kent National (formerly Moatlands). There are still too many golf courses for the level of demand. As a result joining fees are often disregarded and itinerant golfers have become a modern day phenomenon.

Continued investment

Despite the economic background, investment continued throughout this time both on and off the course. The main lounge was re-decorated and the ground-floor murals were professionally cleaned and renovated. The positioning of them in the lounge was then changed to give the room a more modern look. The men's locker-room was refurbished in the Autumn of 2005 at a cost of £62,000, a disabled toilet added and disabled access to the Jubilee Terrace was created in 2006.

On the course the policy of ensuring the Club employed a quality Course Manager continued. There were serious concerns when Peter Gee left the Club (February 2005) as to whether a good enough replacement could be found. These fears proved unfounded as John Donnelly joined CGC and continued to upgrade the quality of the course and its appearance. He had a vision to create a 'little gem' of a course and the Board backed him by upgrading the course machinery. Fairway watering was again considered in 2005 but rejected due to lack of funds. When Donnelly suddenly resigned, there was less angst and John Hunnisett was recruited from The Addington in December 2006. He continues to maintain the now much-praised golf course.

Pointing out detailing in the dining room to the Duke of Gloucester

On 24 September 2008 Prince Richard, Duke of Gloucester visited Camden Place to mark the occasion of completion of the cleaning and restoration of the small murals in the Mixed Lounge. In accordance with protocol, the welcoming committee included the Mayor of Bromley and HM Lord-Lieutenant of Greater London.

139

Self-help

The Putt In Club was an innovation started in 2008 with its raison d'être is to promote and fund projects within the clubhouse for the enjoyment of members and assist the Board in the upkeep of the house. It has approximately 200 members and to date has purchased the chandeliers and lighting for the mixed lounge redecoration, the hall furniture for that refurbishment project, the repair of the settle in the entrance hall and mirrors in the dining room.

One impact of the internet

Professional Jon Bird left the Club in December 2006 to concentrate on an indoor golf coaching business. By that time the internet had become a serious threat to the Professional's traditional source of retail income. Reduced sales of clubs or clothing to the members is a financial headache for any club professional and just one example of technology changing consumer behaviour.

Chris Aked became the Professional early in 2007. The Club now looked at other ways to make the shop work and trialled stocking and operating the shop using a franchise arm of the golf retailer, Nevada Bob. The Professional had a slightly changed package; a negotiated personal financial arrangement with the franchisee plus his teaching earnings and a smaller retainer from the Club (while the franchisee got his retail profits).

Aked moved on to Royal Blackheath GC in January 2008 and CGC appointed David Bicknell as the new Professional under a similar arrangement but by this time the financial storm clouds were gathering over Nevada Bob (UK) Ltd. The arrangement had to be scrapped. David was very popular with the members; he was happy to be the Professional but did not wish to shoulder the retail risks of running the shop.

There were growing concerns about the revolving door nature of the appointments of Professionals. When Paul Eastwood took up the Professional role in May 2010 any concerns melted away. The retail side reverted to the Professional and matters settled down as he became part of a group of professionals who pool resources to give themselves the buying strength to compete. Paul has now been the Club's Professional for eight years and long may it continue. Chislehurst member's benefit from a well-stocked shop and customer service to complement it.

Catering for young and old

Golf clubs are unusual in the diversity of their membership and the challenges faced by different groups. In this period the issues of cost and access were addressed to help two specific membership groups.

Recognition of the difficulties younger people have in paying subscriptions for clubs resulted in a revised and more gradual increase in subscription rates from Junior to Senior Member. In this way younger members did not pay a full subscription until they reached the age of 30.

To help older members golf buggies were finally approved in 2006 after some debate about the safety aspects of some three-wheel, single user models on the undulating course. And perhaps unsurprisingly there was suddenly a need for a buggy shed, which was built in 2009 just inside the staff parking compound to provide security.

2007 and 2008
CGC wins
Business Ladies League

Golf highlights

On the golfing front there was less inter-club success in the second half of this decade. The ladies however recorded their first successes in the Business Ladies League, winning back to back in seasons 2007 and 2008 under the captaincy of Sue Smollett. There were also some notable individual achievements:

- Michael Hamilton lowered the 36–hole amateur course record to 128 on the way to winning the Club Championship in 2008.

- Graham Kerr shot a 61 under winter rules in the January 2009 monthly medal.

- Anthony Tarchetti won the 2008 Pro-Am with a course record 59, with birdies at each of the last five holes.

- Lucy Matthews broke the ladies' course record in October 2009, scoring a remarkable 66 including six birdies.

2009
Ms. L. Matthews
sets new ladies' course
record of 66

The last decade

At the start of 2010 the Board, who were keen on taking big steps towards the future, came up with a strategic plan, laying out capital projects costing about £600,000 and identified ways to raise the required funds. They had already raised the Company's borrowing powers a few years earlier to £500,000.

The new plan was put to the membership in May 2010. There was an enthusiastic debate and the proposals were carried but not by the significant majority the Board felt was appropriate. It may be that the effects of the banking crisis were too fresh in the minds of those present. By December of that year several of the Board stepped down and Michael Lodwig stepped up as the new Chairman.

Mike Lodwig described their approach, *'The new Board sought to build on the work of its predecessors with continuing investment in the clubhouse and course whilst exercising strict financial controls.'*

The ladies' locker room was upgraded as a matter of urgency, whilst the refurbishment of the main hall and stairway required more planning, given its significance and the cost of the project. The billiard-room was redecorated, the exterior of the building was repainted and some roof repairs carried out. After all this work there was little cash to spare for other projects. The Putt In Club and self-help became very useful. The Faber Bar for example was given a significant update in 2014 by the Captain, Phil Matthews, and a band of helpers.

On the course paths were replaced,

improvements made to the irrigation of the 4th and 18th fairways, an additional irrigation tank was installed beside the 18th green, and new equipment purchased including a green iron, which has vastly increased the speed of the greens. In 2015 another bunker programme was started which will continue into the 2020s.

Although Peter Gee had effectively redesigned and created the new 13th hole in 2003/4, the proposal to do something similar to the 7th hole was put out to contract. The project was controversial because 'The Pit' was considered by many to be the signature hole on CGC's compact layout. It still divides opinion, although it has to be said that successive minor alterations had only worsened the appeal of the hole and from a practical perspective it is now playable by golfers of any ability. It also looks great. The honour of being the first to play the hole was auctioned, and Robert Finlay (Captain 2018) paid £100 for that privilege in 2013. Robert unfortunately lost his ball and never completed the hole!

2013
7th hole redesigned

Mike Lodwig had reason to be proud of the progress made. As he put it: '*Throughout this period whilst significant improvements were made to the clubhouse and the course, a surplus of income over expenditure was achieved each year and even more pleasing in the days before the period drew to a close monies totalling nearly £65,000 were received from a refund of VAT from HMRC following settlement of a long-standing claim*'.

Ernest Jones remembered

There was one further addition to the memorabilia in the clubhouse. In 2012 Chris Walker, a member of the Club back in the 1980s, presented us with four clubs inscribed '*Ernest Jones Chislehurst*'. They are displayed in a cabinet near the entrance to the snooker-room.

More inter-club success

Under the captaincy of Colin Chandler, Chislehurst won the Blackheath Trophy again in 2012 at Lamberhurst, whilst Phil G Matthews and his team brought home the West Kent Trophy at Wrotham Heath GC in 2014. Both wins were suitably celebrated back at Camden Place that same evening, and for several days afterwards.

Nurturing the grass roots

Although Chislehurst's membership numbers have held steady, attracting and supporting new golfers is an ongoing challenge for all clubs.

Ernest Jones clubs

The juniors

Chislehurst continues to strive to maintain a healthy junior section. Norman Dyer relaxed after his exertions of the centenary year and then took over from the ladies organising the juniors. He handed the role in 2004 to Phil Matthews (Captain 2014), who passed the responsibility on to Nick Broughton in 2012 and most recently Simon Smollett in 2015. All of them were actively supported by the Professional of the day building on the ethos of teaching introduced to Chislehurst by Ernest Jones and Sydney Mason. It continued to produce winning teams, with the juniors being victorious in the Srixon Junior Foursomes in 2015, the Langley Park Youth League (2016) and the Shooters Hill Youth Cup in 2017, the latter being Chislehurst's first win in this event is it's 41 year history.

Jon Chapman and Suzanne Doyle (Captains 2017) decided to commit a portion of the charity monies raised in their year of captaincy to provide bursaries for young people who may not otherwise be able to afford to pay for clubs, lessons and subscriptions. Two juniors have benefitted from this scheme so far. They are both local and both were referred to us by existing members. This programme of support continues.

The Academy

The Academy was perhaps the most imaginative innovation during recent years. Its purpose is to create a short-term collegiate environment for adults who are new to golf, allowing them access to teaching and to the golf course at preferential rates but with some limited access. It has been successful from the outset, particularly with ladies and many have now graduated to full membership.

2016 onwards

The Board changed again when Michael Lodwig stepped down. It is now chaired by John Couch, with some hands-on management by Vice Chairman, Simon Gander. They took the reins at the same time as the elegant, automated new entrance gates became operational, some 74 years after the Strode gates were removed to help the war effort. They are perhaps an outward sign of a continued move towards improving the quality and feel of the wonderful facilities that are on offer inside.

In the office Mark Hickson, a most amiable and likeable General Manager with a relaxed front of house style, moved on in 2017 but only down the road to Royal Blackheath GC. And as change seemed to be in the air, Mark was succeeded by the Club's first lady General Manager, Ms Juli Carpenter.

Liam Burns, Club Champion 2017 with Captains Chapman and Doyle

2018
Liam Burns
sets new course record
of 58

Liam Burns

Liam Burns joined the Club in 2016. Playing off a useful +4 handicap he had already won the Kent Amateur Championship twice. He had been part of the England elite squad in 2009 with the likes of Tommy Fleetwood, Tyrell Hatton, Eddie Pepperell and Andy Sullivan. He then had a short dalliance with the professional game from 2011–2014.

Liam instantly made an impact at Chislehurst, winning the Club Championship by smashing the record score with an impressive 66 + 60 = 126. The second round tied the course record set in 2012 and he became the first member to shoot a 60 in competition around this course. Liam has retained that championship in each of the two subsequent years. In October 2018 he became the sole holder of the course record, scoring 58.

Whilst a member with the Club he has also won the Waterford 2016 & 2017, The Bishops Bowl 2017, Darwin Plate 2017, and the Watson Trophy 2018, whilst he finished in the top 25 in the English Amateur Oder of Merit in all 3 years..........and he won the Kent Amateur Championship for a third time in 2018.

The Andrews brothers with Captain Robert Finlay 2018

The Brothers

Peter Boult had effectively retired from running his brain-child by the millennium and handed the organisation of the Brothers back to the office. By then the three day competition had been reduced to a two day affair because of the restriction on members playing rights on that weekend. It was taken over by David Hatton who ran it until heart surgery prompted another change and Colin Chandler stepped into the breach.

The Brothers themselves presented the Club with a bench to mark their appreciation on the CGC centenary, which proudly stands beside the 8th tee. They also presented Peter Boult with a golden putter. The Young pairing, Robert and Paul, won the event consecutively four times from 2000, ended by the home grown Hattons in 2004. Since then Robert and Stephen Finlay, another home pairing, have also won four times.

The competition celebrated its 40th anniversary in 2018, with yet another home pairing, Ed and Toby Andrews being victorious. It is quite amazing that pairs return year after year from far afield to play, with some having played nearly every year since the original event back in 1979. Peter Boult would have been thrilled.

Social shenanigans

The wonderfully colourful social side of the Club has characterised its 125 years with fun days, informative talks, bridge suppers, Club nights, concerts, restaurant evenings, comedy nights, B.B.Qs. parties and balls.. The children have Easter egg hunts and Christmas parties, games events ...simply too many to mention but all great fun.

147

Giving with fun

Social and golf activity have often been tied into fund-raising events or activities. Over recent years there have been annually nominated Captains' charities. One regular and ever popular Quiz Night masterminded by Irene Wilson and her team has raised over £65,000 over 16 years.

The generosity of members has bought wheel-chairs and granted special wishes for children, supported cancer research, the local Chartwell Trust, hospice services, the British Heart Foundation, bought a defibrillator for the Club and much more.

There have been raffles and sponsored walks and shaves, penalties on the course and silent auctions but in 2008 our ladies raised the bar (and a few eyebrows) by producing a risqué calendar (from an idea developed into a feature film, The Calendar Girls, in 2003). They raised nearly £2,500 for the Royal British Legion.

151

The weather

It would perhaps be un-British not to mention the weather. Since the millennium there have been good summers, bad summers and indifferent summers, harsh winters and mild winters. Two recent years have been worthy of comment. In 2012, after a very dry winter, a hosepipe ban was imposed by Thames Water on 5 April. Chislehurst GC got some exemption because of the national open event run at Club, namely The Brothers. A spokesman for Thames Water announced at the time of the ban that 'there was no likelihood of the ban being lifted during the entire summer due to the low reservoir levels, even if it rained every day.' ....The ban was lifted on 13 June after torrential and persistent rain produced the wettest April and May since records began over 100 years before. The wet weather continued throughout the summer.

The summer of 2018 was the opposite and rivalled 1976 for heat and drought conditions. Strangely the 2018 summer followed an odd, maybe unique, effect of the weather. The Dinner Foursomes had on occasion been cancelled within living memory due to rain. It had never been cancelled before, as far as can be ascertained, due to snow. In 2018 that finally happened. However three intrepid captains Robert Finlay, Ruth Griffin and Arran Khanna refused to be beaten and marched out at the appointed time and fulfilled the tradition of driving-in to mark the beginning of their year in office, watched by more members that could seriously have been expected.

The three Captains at the wintery 2018 drive in

Change is inevitable

Change has been a constant over 125 years of CGC and responding to changing needs has been an ongoing challenge for successive managements and boards. There have been social, economic, and technological changes influencing how people want to play and enjoy the amenities of club life.

Recently clubs have experimented with basic fees being topped up with a pay-and-play option but it is time, as much as money, which is today's scarce resource. Clubs are offering 9–hole alternative competitions to provide options for those time-poor members. The analogue age has already given way to a digital and mobile revolution and the world is a smaller place as a result. With social media and the internet, there is an inherent capacity to make everyone and everything available 24/7. There is a whole new canvas on which to work and new expectations from current and prospective members.

The pressures for change are not new and Chislehurst Golf Club has responded perhaps a little slowly and sometimes a bit reluctantly, but change it has! In 1996 for example the ladies changed their rules to allow for a vice-captain. The men noted this development and cogitated, deliberated and then acted swiftly by following suit……..in 2018.

As a result of that change, final words can come from the two current vice-captains, Peter Unwin and Kathy Buckley, to focus on the future for Chislehurst Golf Club.

153

Looking forward

We all recognise that we are privileged to be members of Chislehurst, with our wonderful course and a magnificent clubhouse. But as we tee off on the 1st, or as we enjoy a summer evening drink on the terrace, we don't often think of those in whose footsteps we follow, golfers of all abilities over 125 years and the many, including royalty and nobility, who have been entertained in Camden Place over three centuries. Angela Hatton and Steve Jones have done an incredible job through this book in giving us a true insight into that past which is our history.

Both Camden Place and the course have seen many changes in their time, as occupants and decades have passed by. Any organisation has to move with the times and we live in a very different world from that of even our centenary, twenty five years ago. The boundaries between work and leisure time have become blurred and family responsibilities are now shared much more equitability. Both of these trends have put pressure on the traditional golf club model, particularly for young working parents. Our attractive but short course becomes an advantage in a world where the three-hour round is at a premium. And we can be proud of the increase in the number of our younger members and of the success of our Academy, particularly in the ladies' section.

We are lucky to have a course that golfers of all ages and abilities can play and a venue located in a beautiful and very tranquil corner of Chislehurst. CGC can be enjoyed by all generations of a family, a club that provides opportunities for developing lasting friendships and offers an inclusive social calendar enjoyed with the magnificent Camden Place as a backdrop. If you haven't visited the house or played our course we invite you to do so, you will be warmly welcomed.

As your Captain and Ladies' Captain for 2019 we urge you to help us celebrate our 125th anniversary by filling our golfing and social events with members, families and friends and help us ensure that the next chapter in the history of our Club and Camden Place is as exciting as any in the past.

Kathy Buckley

Peter Unwin

2044
To the next 25 years

Officers

Chairman

1898-1905	J. Dun
1906-1924	A. Travers Hawes
1924-1939	J. White
1940-1953	H. Crewdson-Howard
1953-1959	R. Travers Hawes
1960-1961	H.W. O'Brien
1962-1965	J. Stratford
1966-1973	A.J. Todman
1974-1984	H.S. Greensted
1985-1991	P.D. Gibson
1991-1995	P.J. Downs
1995-1998	A.L.R. Hawkins
1998-2004	E.M. Hollingswoth MBE
2004-2010	J.M.B. Lenton
2010-2016	M.S. Lodwig
2016-2017	D.S.M Hatton
2017-	J.L. Couch

Club Secretary

1894	E. Satow Allen
(c) 1898	Thomas Gilroy
1900	A.W.T. Minshin
1903	George W. Hamilton
1906	J. Ross Divett
1907	Capt. H.R. Cobbett
1908	Evan Edwards
1914	H. Somers James (Honorary)
1917	H.R. Cobbett (Honorary)
1919	Percy Scott
1930	George Ferguson
1947	Capt. E.W. Sinclair
1958	Col. Alexander Blair
1959	Major S.P. Briggs
1960	Air Commodore S.A.C. Gray
1962	Wing Commander Waddington
1962	A.T. Balls
1965	Major S.P. Briggs (Honorary)
1966	G.W. Minney
1966	L.C. Jackson
1970	J.A. Irons
1979	N.E. Pearson
2001	D. Bowles
2003	P. J. Foord
2008	M. Hickson
2017	Ms J Carpenter

Club Captain

1894	J. Dun
1895	M.R. Smith
1896	C.E. Hambro
1897	A. Marshall
1898	D.S. Hindmarsh
1899	T.R. Hewitt
1900	E. Devonshire
1901	N. Balme
1902	R.H. Dun
1903	H. Somers James
1904	C.E. Dick
1905	E. Roger Owen
1906	N. Stanhope Stott
1907	J. Ford
1908	J. Margetson
1909	G.T. Hawes
1910	N.P. Tod
1911	W. Clark Pettigrew
1912	D.J. Williams
1913	H. O'Brien
1914-17	A. N. Lubbock
1918	R. A. Brown
1919	F.L. Pattison
1920	H.G. Sicklemore
1921	R.E. Hedderwick
1922	H.T. Holdron
1923	J. White
1924	H.T.O. Leggatt
1925	C.E. Hue Williams
1926	H.C. Howard

1927	R.H. Marriott	1961	L.H. Gilbert	1990	W.J. Marle
1928	H. W .O'Brien MC TD	1962	Brig. F. Pocock OBE MC	1991	W.M. Mitchell
1929	W. L. Hartley	1963	A.I. Todman	1992	D.W.R. Rutnam
1930	C. P. Heseltine	1964	E. Wassell-Smith	1993	D.F. Studley
1931	L.G. Jackson	1965	A.L.R. Hawkins	1994	N.J. Dyer
1932	Col. H.W. Hill. CMG DSO	1966	J. Stratford	1995	M.E. Collett
1933	C.E. Fletcher	1967	C.A.R. Lawrence	1996	R.C. Purkiss
1934	G.G.G. Loch	1968	J. R. Rhodes	1997	R.P.M Philips
1935	E. Ford Duncanson DSC JP	1969	Dr. I. Kelsey Fry	1998	D.J. Spragg
1936	N. Christopherson MC	1970	H.S. Greensted	1999	K.J. Stone
1937	F.E. Pratten		J.B. Pinchard	2000	A.C. Keenan
1938	F. S. Marsh	1971	M.C. Bollon	2001	G.S. Caldwell
1939-41	C. Mitchell	1972	M.S. Lake	2002	H.A. Shaw
1942-45	C.E. Fletcher	1973	Dr. J.D. Williams	2003	J.E.A Walker
1946	R.T. Hawes	1974	D. F. Sim	2004	D.S.M. Hatton
1947	R.E. Attenborough	1975	C.W. Couch	2005	D.R. Smith
1948	Lt. Gen. F.G. Wrisberg CBE CB	1976	I.D. Todman	2006	G. Wilson
1949	G.P. Jackson	1977	Lt. Col. L.F. Rigden TD	2007	R. Pollard
1950	T.K. Collett	1978	H.C. Westall	2008	S.J. Ryle
1951	P.C. Lamb KC	1979	P.W.S. Boult TD	2009	M.S. Lodwig
1952	R.J. Attenborough	1980	Col. R.A. Pont DSO OBE	2010	L.R. Sampson
1953	A. J. Cridlan	1981	R.H. Furniss	2011	R.J. March
1954	Dr. A.E. O'Donnell MBE	1982	P.D. Gibson	2012	W.H. Edwards
1955	M.S. Gray	1983	T.A. Harrison	2013	P. Skinner
1956	E.W. Paffard	1984	Dr. M Hatton	2014	P.J.F. Matthews
1957	C.W.Astell	1985	E.M. Hollingsworth	2015	E.H. Colburn
1958	Brig. N.C. Dobbs	1986	A.R. Armitage	2016	A.C. Baldwin
1959	Lt. Gen. Sir F.G. Wrisberg CBE CB	1987	D.P. Johnson	2017	J. S. Chapman
		1988	D.E.R. Kerr	2018	R. Finlay
1960	D.R.Lang	1989	P.J. Downs	2019	P. Unwin

Lady Captain

1935	Mrs T.H. Jackson
1936	Miss J. Mansell
1937	Miss R. Brown
1938	Miss B.M. Jackson
1939-41	Mrs R.T. Hawes
1942-45	Mrs R.T. Hawes
1946	Mrs L. Simpson
1947	Mrs J.K. Wells
1948	Mrs. R.D. Lang
1949	Mrs H.C. Pyne
1950	Mrs. M. R. Marshall
1951	Mrs A.E. O'Donnell
1952	Mrs E. W. Ganderton
1953	Mrs A. J. Somers
1954	Mrs. E.B. Wrighton
1955	Mrs J.R.G. Barter
1956	The Hon Mrs R.C. Hughes
1957	Mrs A. W. Ingliss
1958	Mrs G.R. Eddy
1959	Mrs C.W Astell
1960	Mrs K.H. Nalder
1961	Mrs E.M. Kemp
1962	Mrs E.M Caswell
1963	Mrs A.C. Glendinning
1964	Mrs N.C. Dobbs
1965	Mrs G. Mason
1966	Mrs A. L Fielding
1967	Mrs K.C. Jones
1968	Mrs J.N. Sutton
1969	Mrs H. P. B. Cox
1970	Mrs J. Stratford
1971	Mrs S.P. Briggs
1972	Mrs R. Gooda
1973	Mrs H.R.D. Jarman
1974	Mrs P.G.L. Bates
1975	Miss L. Frenkel
1976	Mrs M. C. Bollan
1977	Mrs A. L. R. Hawkins
1978	Mrs P. W. S. Boult
1979	Mrs V Gough- Cooper
1980	Mrs H.P. Clifford
1981	Mrs C.T. Stacey
1982	Miss J. Austen
1983	Mrs W. J. Marle
1984	Mrs P. D. Gibson
1985	Mrs M. Robertson
1986	Mrs P Thomas
1987	Mrs S. F. Turner
1988	Mrs G. J. M. Cook
1989	Mrs B. M. Hatton
1990	Mrs L.F. Furniss
1991	Mrs E.J. Hoskin
1992	Miss J.F. Douglas
1993	Mrs M. Luckham-Down
1994	Mrs J.E. Kerr
1995	Mrs J.S. Philips
1996	Mrs E.A. Armitage
1997	Mrs M. Pattrick
1998	Mrs F.A. Clark
1999	Dr H. Reed
2000	Mrs M. Sellar
2001	Mrs S.C. Allwood
2002	Mrs S. Walker
2003	Mrs G.M. Evans
2004	Mrs J. M. Smith
2005	Mrs A. S. Hamill
2006	Mrs P. A Warren
2007	Mrs S. J. Sampson
2008	Mrs J.E. Broadfield
2009	Mrs A.L. Edwards
2010	Miss J. Palmer
2011	Dr J.L. Lamb
2012	Mrs J. M. Walker
2013	Dr S.J. Matthews
2014	Mrs M.A. Moger
2015	Dr R.A. Sykes
2016	Mrs M. E. Unwin
2017	Ms S. Doyle
2018	Ms R. Griffin
2019	Ms K. Buckley

Junior Captain

1979	D. Adair
1980	P.J. Denvir
1981	Miss H. Turner
1982	S.M. Gander
1983	C. Porter
1984	T. Hollingsworth
1985	N. Lake
1986	R. Kelly
1987	R. Williams
1988	Barnes
1989	D. Winter
1990	K. Powell
1991	T.J. Spragg
1992	M.C. Wake
1993	G.B. Caldwell
1994	R. Moger
1995	D.C. Keenan
1996	J.A.R. Clinton
1997	M.W.R. Edwards
1998	N.J. Broughton
1999	N.J. Broughton
2000	M. Allocca
2001	C.K. Aked
2002	L. Lee
2003	G.W. Townsend
2004	M. Forbes
2005	M. Partridge
2006	M. Partridge
2007	J. Forde
2008	J. Osborne
2009	J. Kenny
2010	Miss L. Matthews
2011	D. Watson
2012	E.W. Holmans
2013	E. W. Holmans
2014	A.J. Willsmer
2015	A.J Willsmer
2016	T. Andrews
2017	J. French
2018	A.Khanna
2019	L.Pilcher

Club Professional

1894-1899	Dan Bryson
1899-1902	Robert Munro
1902-1910	Jack Youds
1910-1924	Ernest Jones
1924-1931	Alf Bunce
1931-1938	A.G. Wallis
1938-1974	Sydney Mason
1974-1978	David Pratt
1979-1982	Keith MacDonald
1982-1988	Andrew Thompson
1989-1993	Stuart Corstorphine
1993-2001	Mark Lawrence
2001-2006	John Bird
2007-2008	Chris Aked
2008-2010	David Bicknell
2010-	Paul Eastwood

Competition Winners

A list of past winners for the Club competitions is available on the CGC website.

The only thing
a golfer needs
is more daylight

Ben Hogan